Freethought
in the
United States

FREETHOUGHT IN THE UNITED STATES

A Descriptive Bibliography

MARSHALL G. BROWN
and
GORDON STEIN

GREENWOOD PRESS
Westport, Connecticut • London, England

Library of Congress Cataloging in Publication Data

Brown, Marshall G., 1906-
  Freethought in the United States.

  Includes indexes.
  1. Free thought—Bibliography. 2. United States—
Religion—Bibliography. I. Stein, Gordon, joint author. II. Title.
Z7765.B67 [BL2710]   016.211'4'0973   77-91103
ISBN 0-313-20036-X

Library of Congress Catalog Card Number: 77-91103
ISBN: 0-313-20036-X

First published in 1978

Greenwood Press, Inc.
51 Riverside Avenue, Westport, Connecticut 06880

Printed in the United States of America
10 9 8 7 6 5 4 3 2 1

Contents

Preface

Freethought may be defined as thought which is free of dogmatic assumptions (usually those of religious dogma) and which seeks the answers to all questions through rational inquiry. As such, it includes atheism, rationalism, and secular humanism. More importantly, the term encompasses the writings of freethinkers on subjects outside of religion, that is, the world view of freethinkers which followed from their outlook on religion. While in their day many of their ideas were heretical or radical, today they are commonly accepted (e.g., birth control, evolution, women's rights, separation of church and state, abolition of slavery). Moreover, most of the more liberal forms of Christianity and Judaism now preach what freethinkers were condemned for advocating 100 years ago. Therefore, through the history of freethought we are studying the origins and early advocates of many of the ideas that have shaped our modern world. For example, the freethought movement has been a constant and steadfast force for maintaining and strengthening the basic constitutional principles upon which the government of the United States was founded.

If the aims of the organized freethought movement (after its post-Deist beginnings) were to be formulated into one concise statement, perhaps the movement's own "Nine Demands of Liberalism" would serve best. This statement was first published in Francis Ellingwood Abbot's *Index* in 1872. The demands were:

1. No longer exempt churches and other ecclesiastical property from taxation.
2. Discontinue the employment of chaplains by the U.S. government, paid by public money.

3. Discontinue all public appropriations for sectarian educational and charitable institutions.

4. Abolish all religious services sustained by the U.S. government, especially the reading of the Bible in the public schools.

5. Discontinue appointments by the president and state governors of religious feasts and festivals.

6. Abolish the judicial oath and substitute simple affirmation.

7. Repeal all laws enforcing "Christian morality" instead of "natural morality" (e.g., blasphemy laws).

8. Repeal all laws directly or indirectly enforcing the observance of Sunday as the Sabbath.

9. Grant no privilege or advantage to the Christian religion or to any other religion in the constitutions of the United States or of the states, and administer the government on a purely secular basis.

In the approximately 100 years since these demands were first listed, six of the nine (numbers 3, 4, 6, 7, 8, and 9) have been obtained to some degree, while only three (1, 2, and 5) have never come to pass. The chaplain issue would have been resolved long ago, except that no one has been found who has the status to sue as an offended party. At the time the demands were first put forth, not even the most optimistic freethinker would have guessed that two-thirds would one day be satisfied.

The principles of free press, free speech, the separation of church and state, the right to religious belief or unbelief—these have been the goals which freethinkers have sought and defended. The struggle to obtain and secure these liberties has been fought by a few brave men and women at great personal cost to themselves. In this volume we have tried to tell their story and to make it easier for others to expand upon our modest beginnings.

The definitive history of freethought in the United States has not yet been written. This "guidebook" through the maze of a previously uncharted area of publishing should prove useful to those future investigators who attempt to examine more fully what we have found to be one of the most neglected, yet fascinating, areas of U.S. history. We have continually been surprised to discover that America's freethinkers clearly expressed, often for the first time, many of our current ideas about the world.

With the increased organization and accessibility which this bibliography gives to the field of American freethought, it can now be hoped that other writers on American social and intellectual history will no longer be able to overlook freethought as a legitimate subdivision of the fields of intellectual and social history. Obviously, this should not be interpreted as a blanket indictment of previous social historians, for if *all* had been negligent, there would have been few books for us to describe.

This bibliography gathers into one volume the names of the books and their authors which collectively tell the story of freethought in the United States from before the American Revolution to the present day, or from Ethan Allen to Madalyn Murray O'Hair. Included are the names of the leading personalities of the freethought movement, the organizations they founded to further their cause, and the magazines they established to propagandize. Some attention is also given to freethought publishing in the United States, and books dealing with freethought history and biography are listed.

The development of freethought among America's ethnic groups is discussed in Appendix I. The second appendix lists the major freethought collections in U.S. and Canadian universities and public libraries. They are included because, in many cases, actual copies of the books described are quite difficult to locate, even within large library collections. Many libraries have neglected or have avoided obtaining the important books on freethought. Appendix III lists unpublished theses and dissertations that discuss freethought or are biographies of freethinkers. Appendix IV reviews freethought in Canada. The Addendum lists recently published titles and those overlooked until after the numbering system was completed.

The present work attempts to fill a large and important gap in the organization of the field of U.S. freethought literature. In addition to identifying important works in the area, it attempts to describe and evaluate them, and to place them in proper context in the field of freethought as a whole. No comparable work exists.

This book is not designed to eliminate the need to consult the books described. Rather, it is a guide through the tangle of small, short-lived publishers, scattered library holdings, and unfortunately forgotten men and women who fought courageously for what they, and later most of the rest of the world, thought was true.

The book is roughly chronological in format and is divided into four major sections: "The Rise and Decline of Deism," covering the period from about 1750 to about the time of Thomas Paine's death in 1809; "Popular Freethought," covering the period from about 1825 until the time of the Civil War; "The Golden Age of Freethought," covering the period from the Civil War until the death of Robert G. Ingersoll in 1899; and "Freethought in the Twentieth Century."

Occasionally, some of the bibliographical material does not fit neatly into these time boundaries, thereby requiring some repetition. Usually, a cross-reference is given to direct the reader to additional information about a given subject.

Each section is divided into two distinct parts—the narration and the bibliography. Hence, those who are interested solely in the bibliography need not plow through excess verbiage, while those interested only in the descriptive aspects need not be distracted by complex citations. Of necessity, some titles do appear in the narrative. Titles are assigned a number alphabetically by author in each section. The numbering is consecutive, starting with the Introduction. In the bibliographical part of each section, all the titles cited for the first time appear in numerical sequence. Many entries are annotated.

Some of the books listed in the bibliography have had more than one edition, and some many editions. Since to list all of these editions would be beyond the scope of the bibliography, in most cases only the first edition is listed. Occasionally, where we feel that circumstances merit it, we list the first British and the first American edition, or the first edition (when published initially in a foreign language) and the first English translation.

This work is not intended to be an exhaustive listing of all the free-thought books that were ever published (there were thousands). Rather, it concentrates on listing and discussing the important books on the history of freethought in the United States, plus the important periodicals, organizations, and personalities of that movement. From that beginning, it should be fairly easy for anyone to identify many of the freethought publications we felt were not important enough to include in the present volume.

As is true of works dealing with sweeping fields of thought, this bibliography has some limitations. We have had to make some definitions (see Glossary of Terms) and some exclusions. For example, we excluded all publications whose primary aim was political and not anti-religious or freethought; even though the editorial policy or content of such publications contained some elements of freethought. Many of these publications are socialist, anarchist, libertarian, and communist in orientation and are already covered in existing bibliographies. On the other hand, we included a number of titles whose primary aim was historical or philosophical scholarship (and not the promulgation of freethought per se) on the basis that they were not promoting another system of fixed beliefs (political, economic, or social).

As described above, we have not included periodicals whose chief concern was the exposition of such political/economic systems as anarchism, libertarianism, socialism, or communism. In Appendix I, however, we had to bend this rule slightly. Many of the U.S. ethnic free-thought movements themselves mixed politics with their freethought. They were often freethought/socialist movements; in such cases, we have stated this fact.

In a work involving as much detail and labor as the present one, errors are bound to escape unnoticed. We have checked each factual statement and date several times, but if any errors or important omissions have been made, we would greatly appreciate being notified of them.

Marshall G. Brown
Gordon Stein, Ph.D.

Acknowledgments

Many people helped us with this book. While we cannot list all of them, or all of the libraries where we received prompt and efficient attention, we would like to single out the following for special mention: *The American Rationalist* for permission to reprint portions of an earlier draft of part of this material, the Library of Congress, Enoch Pratt Free Library, Ohio State University, Northwestern University, University of Wisconsin, State Historical Society of Wisconsin, University of Minnesota and especially its Immigration History Research Center, Balzekas Library of Lithuanian Culture, Polish National Museum, the Czechoslovak Society of America, Western Reserve Historical Society, Jewish Theological Seminary, Spertus College of Judaica, American Jewish Historical Society, Columbia University, New York Public Library, University of Chicago and University of Michigan.

Among the individuals, we would like to thank Dina Abramowicz, Arnold Barton, Michael Brook, Victor Cejka, Joseph Chada, Lillian Chorvat, Ellen Dunlap, Joe Dwyer, Ernest Espelie, D. M. Farris, Adina Feldstern, Robert Gokovich, John J. Grabowski, Henry Haldeman, Albert Hirsch, Walter Hoops, Zdeněk Hruban, Lloyd Hüstvedt, Esther Jerabek, Mike Karni, Ralph McCoy, Russell Maylone, Mary Molik, Phil Mooney, Halyna Myroniuk, Vojtěch Nevlud, Arthur Puotinin, Darryl Rotman, Lynn Schweitzer, Nathan Simons, George H. Smith, Timothy Smith, Dorothy Swanson, Robert Tibbetts, Ed Weber, and Erwin Welsch.

Freethought
in the
United States

Introduction

An author or subject bibliography is an attempt to bring order to an area of publishing where there formerly was disorder. The present volume is no exception to this idea.

Some areas of publishing exhibit more disorder than others. The field of freethought, rationalist, and atheist publications has until now been among the most disordered, partly because there have been very few published bibliographies in this field. There are a few exceptions. The Russian freethought literature is well organized, with a number of published bibliographies in Russian. There is a bibliography of the Deist literature in all languages (up to 1765), entitled *Freydenker Lexicon* (17). A published library catalog which thoroughly covers the early Deist literature in the large McAlpin Collection at Union Theological Seminary in New York City was published in five volumes in the 1920s (19). Finally, Karl Becker's *Freigestige Bibliographie* (5) is a good bibliography of German freethought books (in German), but it does a poor job on the English language books it covers.

The British literature is better covered in author bibliographies. There is a good bibliography of George Jacob Holyoake (20) by C.W. F. Goss, and there is a fair bibliography of Annie Besant (7), the free-thinker/theosophist, compiled by Theodore Besterman. A fairly complete checklist of Charles Bradlaugh's publications is found at the back of David Tribe's *President Charles Bradlaugh, M.P.* (42).

A few catalogs of freethought libraries in England also exist, and they can serve to help organize the literature of the field. An example is the *Catalogue of the Library of the Rationalist Press Association* (12). There is also a fine series of ten published catalogs of the British former freethought bookdealer, David Collis, that were issued in the late 1960s.

The French freethought literature is represented bibliographically by an author bibliography of Baron d'Holbach entitled *Bibliographie*

Descriptive des Écrits du Baron d'Holbach (43) by Jeroom Vercruysse
and by a bibliography on modern French atheism entitled *L'Athéisme
dans le Monde Moderne* (13), compiled by Bernadette Chevalier and
written from a Catholic viewpoint.

Very little has been done on American freethought or American
freethinkers. One of the present authors (GS) did a bibliography of
Robert G. Ingersoll several years ago entitled *Robert G. Ingersoll:
A Checklist* (39). There are no U.S. freethought subject bibliographies
as such, although several books [e.g., Sidney Warren's *American Freethought, 1860-1914* (44)] do contain good bibliographies for the
periods they cover. The situation is so bad that perhaps the finest
existing "bibliography" of U.S. freethought is the auction sale catalog
of the great Truth Seeker Company sale of 1950. Copies of this catalog are extremely hard to obtain, and, even if obtained, provide only
an incomplete author and title list.

A Critical Bibliography of Religion in America (10) by Nelson R.
Burr is a companion set to the present volume. Although Burr's volumes do contain sections on rationalism, atheism, Deism, freethought,
Ethical Culture, skepticism, and secularism, their coverage is fragmentary. Those sections appear to have been written by someone
who obviously did not know or feel comfortable with the literature
of these fields. These sections also contain a large number of errors
(mostly of omission); such errors no doubt resulted from the author's
unfamiliarity with and lack of perspective in the area.

We have previously mentioned that the definitive history of freethought in the United States has not yet been written. If such a book
is ever undertaken, however, a model does exist: the two two-volume
works by John Mackinnon Robertson entitled *A History of Freethought,
Ancient and Modern, to the Period of the French Revolution* (34)
and *A History of Freethought in the Nineteenth Century* (35). While
these two works are very scholarly, they merely skim over freethought
in the United States.

Some excellent studies of certain periods of the freethought
movement in the United States have been written. *Republican Religion*
(21) by Adolph Koch and *Deism in Eighteenth Century America* (27)
by Herbert M. Morais are fine works on the Deist period. *Popular
Freethought in America, 1825-1850* (29) by Albert Post is a most
thorough study of the period from shortly after Thomas Paine's death
to shortly before the Civil War. *American Freethought, 1860-1914*
(44) by Sidney Warren covers the period when Robert G. Ingersoll
was the most prominent and influential freethinker. *Fifty Years of Freethought* (23) by George E. Macdonald is the story of the freethought

magazine, *The Truth Seeker,* from its founding in 1873 until 1925; Macdonald pretty well covers the history of freethought in the United States during this period.

Four Hundred Years of Freethought (30) by Samuel Porter Putnam is a monumental book written by one of the outstanding freethinkers of the late nineteenth century. It is a study of freethought from the time of Columbus to the end of the nineteenth century. Although it is worldwide in scope and largely biographical in approach, it is uneven in its treatment. It could not be called a work of deep scholarship, although it is one of the best books on the history of freethought, particularly in the United States. It often goes into meticulous detail on one subject, while skimming lightly over a more important one. An inadequate and somewhat biased treatment of freethought in the United States is *The Infidel: Freethought and American Religion* (26) by Martin E. Marty.

The only encyclopedia on freethought worthy of mention is Joseph McCabe's *A Rationalist Encyclopedia* (25), which contains 1,800 articles on religion, philosophy, ethics, and science.

There are many biographical books (6, 16, 22, 24, 30, 32, 37, 39, 40, 45, and 46) which deal with many of the men and women who contributed to the growth of freethought in the United States. Most of these books will be referred to a number of times in subsequent sections. The only two that merit special mention here are Joseph McCabe's *A Biographical Dictionary of Modern Rationalists* (24) and Joseph Mazzini Wheeler's *A Biographical Dictionary of Freethinkers of All Ages and Nations* (45).

Finally, some books of a general nature (1, 2, 3, 4, 8, 9, 11, 14, 15, 18, 28, 31, 33, 34, 35, 36, 38, and 41) give attention to aspects of freethought in the United States.

BIBLIOGRAPHY

1. Anderson, Paul Russell, and Fisch, Harold Max. *Philosophy in America from the Puritans to William James, With Representative Selections.* New York: D. Appleton-Century Co., 1939. Discusses the contributions of the following (among others) to American thought, plus some representative selections from their writings: Benjamin Franklin, Ethan Allen, Thomas Jefferson, Thomas Cooper, Ralph Waldo Emerson, and John Fiske.

2. Angoff, Charles (as Richard W. Hinton). *Arsenal for Skeptics.* New York: Alfred A. Knopf, 1934. A short sampler of freethought

literature. Begins with a textual analysis of the Bible and is followed by carefully selected quotations from the writings of the leading agnostic historians, investigators, and scientists, or from other authoritative documents.

3. Barnes, Harry Elmer. *An Intellectual and Cultural History of the Western World.* New York: Cordon Co., 1937. An important study covering the intellectual development of man from ancient times to the present. Of particular interest to freethinkers are Chapter XVIII, "The Growth of Tolerance and Freedom of Thought," and Chapter XIX, "The Revolution in Religious and Ethical Thought." Contains an excellent bibliography.

4. Baumer, Franklin L. *Religion and the Rise of Skepticism.* New York: Harcourt, Brace & Co., 1960. Follows the conflict between faith and doubt from the time of Galileo to the present.

5. Becker, Karl. *Freigeistige Bibliographie.* Stuttgart, W. Germany: Verlag der Freireligiösen Landesgemeinde Wurtemberg, [1971].

6. Bennett, DeRobigne Mortimer. *The World's Sages, Infidels and Thinkers.* New York: D. M. Bennett, 1876. Although this book is over 100 years old, it is still a valuable source of information on freethought. Consists of 1,048 pages, with sketches of 277 personalities, many of whom were freethinkers. Contains 20 sketches of Americans.

7. Besterman, Theodore. *A Bibliography of Annie Besant.* London: Theosophical Society, 1924. Covers both her freethought and most of her theosophical periods.

8. Blau, Joseph, ed. *Cornerstones of Religious Freedom.* Boston: Beacon Press, 1949. Contains fourteen significant documents in the struggle for religious freedom, including Thomas Jefferson's "An Act for Establishing Religious Freedom" (1779); James Madison's "A Memorial and Remonstrance on the Religious Rights of Man" (1784); Richard M. Johnson's "Sunday Observance and the Mail" (1830); Francis Ellingwood Abbot's "Nine Demands of Liberalism" (1872); Benjamin F. Underwood's "From the Practical Separation of Church and State" (1876); and Felix Frankfurter's "Concurring Opinion in the Vashti McCollum Case" (1948).

9. Bratton, Fred Gladstone. *The Legacy of the Liberal Spirit, Men and Movements in the Making of Modern Thought.* New York: Charles Scribner's Sons, 1943. An excellent book tracing the growth of liberalism in religion from the time of Origen to the present. Presents the contributions of Newton, Locke, Voltaire, Hume, Paine, Jefferson, Allen, Parker, Channing, and others to the spirit of liberalism.

10. Burr, Nelson R., in collaboration with the editors, James Ward Smith and A. Leland Jamison. *A Critical Bibliography of Religion in*

America. Princeton, N.J.: Princeton University Press, 1961, 2 vols. For an analysis of this book, see narration above.

11. Bury, John Bagnell. *A History of Freedom of Thought.* London: Williams & Norgate, 1913. First American edition was New York: Henry Holt & Co., 1913. Covers the growth of freethought from the time of ancient Greece to the present. Highly readable, although very little attention given to the United States.

12. *Catalogue of the Library of the Rationalist Press Association.* London: Watts & Co., 1937. Covers philosophy and science as well as freethought.

13. Chevalier, Bernadette. *L'Atheisme dans le Monde Moderne.* Geneva, Switzerland: no publisher, 1969. Mimeograph of thesis from L'Ecole Bibliothécaries.

14. Curti, Merle. *The Growth of American Thought.* New York: Harper & Brothers, 1943. A good general account of intellectual trends in the United States. Of special interest are the chapters entitled "The Rise of the Enlightenment" and "The Expanding Enlightenment."

15. Darrow, Clarence, and Rice, Wallace. *Infidels and Heretics: An Agnostic's Anthology.* Boston: Stratford Co., 1929. A compilation of quotations from many people, expressing the agnostic viewpoint.

16. Eliot, Samuel Atkins. *Heralds of a Liberal Faith.* Boston: American Unitarian Assoc., 1910. Includes outstanding liberal ministers from colonial times down to 1910, among them Ebenezer Gay, Charles Chauncy, Joseph Priestly, James Freeman, Octavius Brooks Frothingham, and Theodore Parker.

17. *Freydenker Lexicon,* compiled by J. A. Trinius. Leipzig, Germany: Berlegts Christoph Gottfried Corner, 1759-1765, 4 vols. Reprinted in 1966 by Botega D'Erasmo, Turin, Italy. Contains a bibliography of the Deist literature in all languages, up to the year 1765.

18. Gaustad, Edwin Scott. *Dissent in American Religion.* Chicago: University of Chicago Press, 1973. Contains an excellent chapter entitled "The Heretics: Sinners Against Society."

19. Gillett, Charles Ripley, ed. *The McAlpin Collection of British History and Theology.* New York: For the Union Theological Seminary, 1927-1930, 5 vols. A detailed bibliographical catalog of one of the largest collections on Deism in the world. Covers only the early period of Deism (1500-1700).

20. Goss, C.W.F. *A Descriptive Bibliography of the Writings of George Jacob Holyoake, With a Brief Sketch of His Life.* London: Crowther & Goodman, 1908.

21. Koch, G. Adolph. *Republican Religion, The American Revolution and the Cult of Reason.* New York: Henry Holt & Co., 1933. Re-

cently reprinted under the new title *Religion of the American Enlighten-ment.* An excellent book on the Deistic period in America, complete with a good bibliography.

22. Kurtz, Paul, ed. *American Thought Before 1900, A Source-book from Puritanism to Darwinism.* New York: Macmillan Co., 1966. Includes a brief biographical sketch of Benjamin Franklin, Thomas Jefferson, Thomas Paine, Ethan Allen, Elihu Palmer, William E. Chan-ning, John Fiske, and others, plus excerpts from their writings.

23. Macdonald, George E. *Fifty Years of Freethought, Being the Story of The Truth Seeker, With the Natural History of Its Third Editor.* New York: Truth Seeker Co., 1929, 2 vols. The story of freethought in the United States from about 1873 to 1925, as seen through the eyes of the editor of *The Truth Seeker* (a leading freethought magazine).

24. McCabe, Joseph. *A Biographical Dictionary of Modern Ra-tionalists.* London: Watts & Co., 1920. A biographical dictionary of freethinkers, containing over 2,000 names, 63 of them Americans. A modified reprint was issued by Haldeman-Julius Publications in Girard, Kansas, in 1945, under the title *A Biographical Dictionary of Ancient, Medieval and Modern Freethinkers.*

25. McCabe, Joseph. *A Rationalist Encyclopedia.* London: Watts & Co., 1948. Contains 1,800 articles on such subjects as religion, philosophy, freethought, ethics, and science.

26. Marty, Martin E. *The Infidel: Freethought and American Reli-gion.* Cleveland: World Publishing Co., 1961. A general history of the conflict between freethought and ecclesiasticism, written with a dis-tinct pro-religious bias.

27. Morais, Herbert M. *Deism in Eighteenth Century America.* New York: Columbia University Press, 1934. A good account of the rise and decline of Deism in America.

28. Muelder, Walter G., and Sears, Laurence. *The Development of American Philosophy.* Boston: Houghton Mifflin Co., 1940. A source-book on the philosophical traditions of our country. Includes the writings of Benjamin Franklin, Thomas Jefferson, Elihu Palmer, Ethan Allen, Theodore Parker, John Fiske, and others.

29. Post, Albert. *Popular Freethought in America, 1825-1850.* New York: Columbia University Press, 1943. An excellent account of the growth and development of freethought in the period covered.

30. Putnam, Samuel Porter. *Four Hundred Years of Freethought.* New York: Truth Seeker Co., 1894. For an analysis of this book, see narration above.

31. Randall, John Herman, Jr. *The Making of the Modern Mind,*

A Survey of the Intellectual Background of the Present Age. Boston: Houghton Mifflin Co., 1926. A comprehensive survey of man's intellectual development in Western civilization. Chapter XIII (entitled "The Religion of Reason") covers the period of the Age of Reason (1650-1800). Chapter XX ("Religion in the Growing World") and Chapter XVIII ("The World Conceived as a Process of Growth and Evolution") cover religion and science in the nineteenth century.

32. Remsburg, John E. *Six Historic Americans.* New York: Truth Seeker Co., 1906. Discusses the religious beliefs of Benjamin Franklin, Thomas Paine, Thomas Jefferson, George Washington, Abraham Lincoln, and Ulysses S. Grant. Must be used with caution as it contains a number of unsupported conclusions.

33. Riley, Isaac Woodbridge. *American Philosophy, The Early Schools.* New York: Dodd, Mead & Co., 1907. An early but excellent study of philosophy in America. One section devoted to the rise and decline of Deism, and another to the prevalence of Deism at various colleges. Discusses Joseph Priestly and Thomas Cooper under the section on materialism.

34. Robertson, John M. *A History of Freethought, Ancient and Modern, to the Period of the French Revolution.* London: Watts & Co., 1936, 2 vols. A meticulous and scholarly study of freethought from its beginnings. Unsurpassed for what it attempts, but weak in its coverage of freethought in the United States.

35. Robertson, John M. *A History of Freethought in the Nineteenth Century.* London: Watts & Co., 1929. American edition published in New York by G. P. Putnam's Sons in 1930 (2 vols.). A chronological continuation of the suberb job begun in no. 34 above. Filled with detail and scholarship, but again, not too thorough on the United States, although there is a chapter on it.

36. Robertson, John M. *A Short History of Freethought, Ancient and Modern.* London: Swan, Sonnenschein, 1899. American edition published in New York by G. P. Putnam's Sons in 1899. The first edition of what was later expanded to four volumes (as nos. 34 and 35 above).

37. Rusterholtz, Wallace P. *American Heretics and Saints.* Boston: Manthorne & Burack, 1938. Largely an anthology of the writings and sayings of such American religious liberals and progressives as Benjamin Franklin, Thomas Paine, Theodore Parker, Robert G. Ingersoll, and Clarence Darrow. Contains an excellent bibliography.

38. Schneider, Herbert Wallace. *A History of American Philosophy.* New York: Columbia University Press, 1946. Perhaps the best history

of philosophy in the United States. Includes a chapter on freethought in the section "The American Enlightenment."

39. Stein, Gordon. *Robert G. Ingersoll: A Checklist.* Kent, Ohio: Kent State University Press, 1969. A bibliography of the works of the man who was probably America's most popular freethinker.

40. Steiner, Franklin. *The Religious Beliefs of Our Presidents.* Girard, Kans.: Haldeman-Julius Publications, 1936. Discusses the religious beliefs of all of our presidents, down to 1936.

41. Tribe, David. *100 Years of Freethought.* London: Elek, 1967. Covers the development of freethought during the past 100 years and deals mostly with British freethought.

42. Tribe, David. *President Charles Bradlaugh, M.P.* London: Paul Elek, 1971. Probably the best biography of England's leading free-thinker, using papers until recently thought to be lost.

43. Vercruysse, Jeroom. *Bibliographie Descriptive des Écrits du Baron d'Holbach.* Paris: Minard, 1971. The first full bibliography of one of France's most outspoken atheists.

44. Warren, Sidney. *American Freethought, 1860-1914.* New York: Columbia University Press, 1943. An excellent account of the growth and development of freethought during the time of Robert G. Ingersoll. Contains an excellent bibliography.

45. Wheeler, Joseph Mazzini. *A Biographical Dictionary of Free-thinkers of All Ages and Nations.* London: Progressive Publishing Co., 1889. One of the early biographical dictionaries of freethinkers and a fine piece of scholarship. Includes a few Americans, such as William Bell, Titus L. Brown, Thomas Hertell, Benjamin Offen, and Charles B. Reynolds.

46. Whittemore, Robert Clifton. *Makers of the American Mind.* New York: William Morrow & Co., 1964. Presents in their own words the essentials of the philosophy of those thinkers whose influence on our culture has been such as to justify calling them "makers of the American mind." Includes Benjamin Franklin, Thomas Jefferson, Ethan Allen, Thomas Paine, Frances Wright, William Ellery Channing, and John Fiske.

1.
★★★★★★★★★★

The Rise
and Decline of Deism

Deism was at its height in England during the first half of the eighteenth century and by the second half had spread to France and even to Germany. In the latter part of the eighteenth century, too, Deism became popular among the intellectual leaders of America and influenced the thinking of our Founding Fathers.

The roots of American freethought go back to Europe and the Enlightment or "Age of Reason" (1650-1800). The Age of Reason can well be considered the beginning of the modern era because most of our present-day thought patterns can be traced to this period. Some of the patterns that characterized the Age of Reason were:

1. The rise of the scientific spirit
2. Belief in reason as a means of solving problems
3. Secularization of learning
4. Growth of democracy
5. Belief in the natural rights of man
6. Belief in the progress and perfectibility of man.

Although he preceded the Enlightenment, Nicholas Copernicus (1473-1543), a Polish astronomer, was one of the first to give impetus to the scientific spirit. Copernicus first established the heliocentric theory of the solar system, a revolutionary idea, that changed man's conception of the universe and as such represented a dangerous challenge to theologians.

The Copernican theory was popularized by an Italian philosopher, Giordano Bruno (1548-1600), who traveled around Europe espousing the theory. Bruno's open rebellion against reactionary aspects of Catholicism brought him into conflict with the Church, and when he returned to Italy, he was seized, turned over to the Inquisition, and finally burned at the stake in 1600. Today he is regarded as one of the heroes of freethought. The truth of Copernicus's theory was confirmed by Tycho Brahe (1546-1601) and Johann Kepler (1571-1630).

The next noteworthy figure in the revolution in astronomy was the Italian Galileo Galilei (1564-1642), who first used the telescope for astronomical observation. His discoveries further confirmed Copernicus's ideas, and since his findings were also contrary to the teachings of the Catholic Church, he too was brought before the Inquisition.

Another precursor of the Enlightenment was Rene Descartes (1596-1650) of France, the founder of modern philosophy. In his *Discourse on Method* (77), he advocated the discarding of all authorities and the acceptance of only those propositions that could be reasonably understood and demonstrated. The first to apply the methods of science to philosophy, Descartes was a great mathematician who prepared the way for Newton's important synthesis.

Thomas Hobbes (1588-1679) of England, a thoroughgoing naturalistic thinker, attempted to outline a universal system of human knowledge which would explain man and society the same way that natural forces are explained. A materialist and a freethinker, Hobbes eliminated the supernatural from his thinking.

Another great contributor to the Age of Reason was Baruch Spinoza (1632-1677), a Portuguese-born Jew, who spent his life in Amsterdam as a lens grinder. Drawing upon the works of Hobbes and Descartes, he worked out a mechanico-naturalistic view of the universe and developed the pantheistic idea in which God and the universe are one.

Two great forerunners of the Enlightenment were the Englishmen John Locke (1632-1704) and Isaac Newton (1642-1727). Locke was the founder of modern empiricism. In his *Essay Concerning Human Understanding* (113), which went through twenty editions in ten years, Locke stated that the mind has no innate ideas, that it is a blank tablet at birth, and all knowledge comes through sense experiences. Locke also led the fight against intolerance and defended reason against faith, his *Letters on Toleration* (114) and *Reasonableness of Christianity* (115) being especially influential.

Isaac Newton, one of the greatest scientists of all time, systematized the achievements of the thinkers who preceded him. By the time he was twenty-four, he had formulated the law of gravitation, the principles of calculus, and the theory of light. Newton arranged in complete mathematical form a mechanical view of nature, and defined the world as a great cosmic machine operating according to perpetual mathematical principles. His great synthesis appeared in his *Principia Mathematica* (122).

During the period of the Enlightenment, there developed a religious attitude that came to be known as Deism, and sometimes as "the religion of reason" or "natural religion." The term *Deist* was first used by Pierre Viret, a Swiss Protestant, to describe those who believed in God but not in the divinity of Jesus.

The growth of Deism during the eighteenth century can be attributed to the following factors: (1) the rationalism of Locke and his school of thought, (2) the Newtonian world-machine, (3) geographical exploration which brought man into contact with other religions, and (4) liberalizing tendencies caused by the endless squabbles among the Christian churches and sects. According to Deism, God was the source of universal law, setting in motion the immutable laws of nature. It was useless to attempt to change laws through prayer or by other means.

The first important Deistic writer was Lord Herbert of Cherbury (1583-1648), an Englishman, who is known as the father of Deism. His *Religion of the Gentiles With the Causes of Their Errors* (98), published in 1645, most fully expresses his Deistic philosophy. Here he established his basic creed: (1) there is one God, (2) He is to be worshiped, (3) man should repent his sins, (4) virtue and piety are the chief part of goodness, and (5) there is reward or punishment in the afterlife. Herbert maintained that these beliefs were held by all men at all times, regardless of race or religion.

Deism in England was popularized by Charles Blount (1654-1693). In his *Oracles of Reason* (60), a collection of his previous writings, he ridiculed religious worship as an invention of the priesthood and condemned the miraculous elements in Christianity as a fabrication.

Later influential Deists in England were John Toland, Anthony Collins, and William Wollaston. Toland (1670-1722), a disciple of Locke, wrote *Christianity Not Mysterious* (156) based on Locke's *Reasonableness of Christianity* (115). Toland's goal was to eliminate the supernatural from Christianity. Collins (1676-1729) attacked the prophecies of the Bible in his *Discourse on the Grounds and Reasons of the Christian Religion* (73). He also wrote *A Discourse of Freethinking* (72), which was a plea for free discussion and for the submission of all religious questions to examination by reason. (Voltaire and Franklin were influenced by this book.) In *The Religion of Nature Delineated* (167), William Wollaston (1660-1724) advanced the idea that a religion of reason is completely adequate to the needs of man and society.

The most important writer of the Deistic school was Matthew Tindal (1657-1733) whose *Christianity as Old as the Creation* (155) was the best statement of Deism. Tindal believed in a God of reason rather than in a jealous, revengeful, vindictive deity. He attempted to show that the teachings of Jesus were the same as those of Deistic and natural religion.

Thomas Woolston (1670-1733), unlike most of the other Deistic writers, wrote for the masses, a fact that made him especially dangerous in the eyes of the clergy. In his six *Discourses on the Miracles of our Savior* (170), Woolston made a violent attack on the miracles of Jesus. His *Discourses* had such a large circulation in England that the clerical authorities, alarmed by his influence, brought charges against him. He was convicted of blasphemy and sentenced to prison.

Another Deist who attempted to appeal to the literate masses was Thomas Chubb (1679-1747). Unlike the other Deists, Chubb himself came from the common people and had little formal schooling. In his *Discourse Concerning Reason* (68), he set forth the nature and adequacy of natural religion. In his *True Gospel of Jesus Asserted* (69), he held that God will judge the world by the eternal principles of right and wrong. Chubb also believed that there was a future state of rewards and punishments and he was opposed to the supernatural elements in Christianity.

Other Deists of this era who contributed to Deistic literature were Dr. Thomas Morgan, Anthony Ashley Cooper (the third Earl of Shaftsbury), Henry St. John Bolingbroke, William Whiston, Peter Annet, and Alexander Pope.

The high tide of Deism in England was from 1700 to 1760. Ultimately, it failed as a religious movement because it was too radical for the devout and too conservative for the radical.

Around 1720 Deism spread to France, where Voltaire (François Marie Arouet, 1694-1778) was its most brilliant exponent. Before Voltaire's time, France's outstanding advocate of the rationalistic spirit was Pierre Bayle (1647-1706). Bayle's *Philosophical Commentary on the Words of Jesus "Compel Them to Come in That My House May Be Full"* (54) expresses his arguments for freethinking and religious toleration. Throughout his writings, Voltaire advocated toleration and defended freethinking. He remained a Deist his entire life.

In England, the rationalistic spirit continued in the form of Deism, while in France rationalism swung all the way to atheism. In France, the atheists made quite different deductions from the Newtonian synthesis: they saw no need for a God in a mechanical, eternal universe.

One of the earliest French atheists, Julien de la Mettrie (1709-1751), developed an atheistic and materialistic philosophy which is embodied in his 1748 publication, *Man A Machine* (108).

Paul Henry Thiry, Baron d'Holbach (1723-1789), a wealthy German who lived in France, was perhaps the most outspoken of a group of atheists or near-atheists who lived and wrote in eighteenth-century France. D'Holbach denied God and immortality; he believed that Newtonian science gave a full and complete explanation of the universe. His views are best expounded in his *Good Sense* (99) and *The System of Nature* (100).

Certainly one of the great achievements of the Enlightenment in France was the *Encyclopedie* (82), written by a brilliant group of rationalists and materialists, including Dennis Diderot (1713-1784), Claude Adrien Helvetius (1715-1771), and Jean le Rond D'Alembert (1717-1783). Diderot was the general editor.

Jean-Jacques Rousseau (1712-1778) was a more moderate Deist than Voltaire, and had a more sensitive and emotional temperament. He believed in God and immortality, but rejected the rites and ceremonies of religion, along with its mysteries and revelations. His principal works in this area are *Emile* (139) and *Social Contract* (140).

The growth of Deism brought a spirited defense of Christianity beginning in 1730. One of the first such defenses was *The Case of Reason, or Natural Religion Fairly Stated* (109) by William Law (1686-1761). Perhaps the best defense of Christianity was written by Bishop Joseph Butler (1692-1752) in his *The Analogy of Religion, Natural and Revealed, to the Constitution and Course of Nature* (65). Butler, like Law, attempted to show that revealed religion was as reasonable as natural religion. A later defense of revealed religion was written by William Paley (1743-1805) in *View of the Evidences of Christianity* (129) and *Natural Theology* (128). Of course, these books produced responses from freethinkers, some of them many years later.

Before discussing Deism in America, one other genius of the Enlightenment should be mentioned, namely David Hume (1711-1776). Hume carried Locke's empiricism to its logical conclusion, pointing out that it is unreasonable to believe anything that cannot be corroborated by disinterested and independent witnesses. He made a scientific study of religion, ridiculed revelation, questioned miracles, and rejected the doctrine of a future life. In his *Dialogues Concerning Natural Religion* (102), Hume demolished the ontological, cosmological, and teleological proofs of the existence of God. Other works dealing with these subjects were his *Treatise on Human Nature* (105), *Philosophical Essays Concerning Human Understanding* (103), and *Essay on Miracles* (104).

Additional information on the European background of Deism in

America may be obtained from the following references: 2, 3, 9, 11, 31, 34, 36, 55, 64, 92, 96, 117, 119, 121, 124, 135, 146, 157, and 162.

* * *

Deism did not reach its high point in America until about 1800 with the activities of Thomas Paine and Elihu Palmer. For the most part, Deism was confined to the educated few, particularly until Paine and Palmer attempted to carry Deism to the masses in the 1790s and early 1800s.

Deism took hold in America as a result of the importation of rationalistic works from England, the introduction of Newtonian science, Locke's empiricism, Voltaire's anti-clericalism, the popularization of the new science in magazines and almanacs, and the appearance of the works of scientists and Deists in colonial libraries.

As noted in the Introduction, the two best studies of Deism in America are *Republican Religion* (21) and *Deism in Eighteenth Century America* (27). They are indispensable to an understanding of freethought during this period in American history.

Benjamin Franklin (1706-1790) was the first notable Deist in America. Born and reared in Boston, he became a Deist by the age of fifteen and remained one the rest of his life, although he attended church and gave financial assistance to different denominations. While employed in London in 1725-1726, he wrote a Deistic pamphlet entitled *Dissertation on Liberty and Necessity, Pleasure and Pain* (91), which is reprinted in *American Philosophy* (33). Franklin also discusses his religious views in his *Autobiography* (90). Late in life, in answer to an inquiry from President Ezra Stiles of Yale concerning his religious beliefs, he wrote:

Here is my creed. I believe in one God, creator of the universe. That he governs it by his Providence. That he ought to be worshiped. That the most acceptable service we render him is doing good to his other children. That the soul of man is immortal, and will be treated with justice in another life respecting its conduct in this. These I take to be the fundamental principles of all sound religion.

(For more detailed accounts of Franklin's religious views, see 49, 89, and 148; references 28, 32, 33, 37, and 38 in the Introduction are also relevant.)

George Washington (1732-1799) was what might be termed a "near-Deist." Although nominally a member of the Anglican church, he abstained from the essential forms and conventions of his creed. Most of his official communications during the Revolution contained no references to the Christan religion. His appeal was customarily made to "Heaven," "Providence," "the Supreme Being," "the supreme disposer of all events," and "the great arbiter of the Universe"—terms commonly used by Deists. The best book on Washington's religious views is *George Washington and Religion* (61). See also references 32, 40, and 76.

Thomas Jefferson (1743-1826), the best known and most prominent Deist of the early national period, was thoroughly familiar with the writings of Voltaire and the English Deists. Jefferson claimed that Jesus was a Deist, but he questioned many of the teachings of Christianity. When he ran for president in 1800, he was called an atheist by his opponents. Jefferson expressed his religious views in many letters written in his later life. A more detailed account of these views may be found in references 76, 78, 86, 87, 97, 106, 107, 110, 141, and 149 below. Also see references 21, 27, 28, 33, 38, 40, and 46.

The three outstanding militant Deists of this period were Ethan Allen, Thomas Paine, and Elihu Palmer, all three of whom expressed their Deistic beliefs in books and who attempted to carry their religious views to the common man.

Ethan Allen (1737-1789) was born in Litchfield, Connecticut. Better known for his leadership of the Green Mountain Boys during the American Revolution, Allen also wrote the first anti-Christian book published in the United States. Influenced by the excesses of the Great Awakening, the Deism of his friend Dr. Thomas Young, and his contact with British and French officers during the Revolution, Allen became a Deist. While he believed in God and immortality, he rejected Christianity. Allen wrote the lengthy and repetitive 477-page volume entitled *Reason the Only Oracle of Man* (51). Allen had difficulty in finding a publisher, but finally succeeded in getting Haswell and Russell of Bennington, Vermont, to print 1,500 copies in 1784. The book was received with enthusiasm by freethinkers and fury by the clergy. The impact of the book was considerably diminished, however, when a fire broke out in the printing house and destroyed many copies. This edition is quite rare today. Several subsequent editions were published in the 1800s.

B. T. Schantz's "Ethan Allen's Religious Ideas" in the *Journal of Religion* (143) is an excellent article on the sources of Allen's religious thinking, as well as a summary of his religious beliefs. For biographies of Allen, see references 93, 101, and 133; see also references 1, 9, 21, 22, 26, 27, and 33.

Thomas Paine (1737-1809) wrote what is perhaps the most famous book in the history of freethought. Born in Thetford, England,

Paine came to America in 1774 at the suggestion of Benjamin Franklin. Paine's *Common Sense* (126) was instrumental in crystallizing the sentiment for American independence, and during the Revolutionary War, he wrote *The Crisis* (127), a series of papers that boosted the morale of Americans when most needed. He returned to Europe in 1787 and was elected to the French National Assembly during the French Revolution. He ultimately lost favor with the leaders of the Revolution and was imprisoned for ten months. Before his imprisonment, he wrote Part I of *The Age of Reason* (125), primarily to combat the spread of atheism. Part II was written after his release from prison. The publication of Part I in 1794 and Part II in 1795 created a sensation in the religious world. The book was widely sold and read in America. Paine returned to the United States in 1802 and spent most of the rest of his life on his farm at New Rochelle, New York, and in New York City.

Paine's religious beliefs as expressed in *The Age of Reason* included the following:

I believe in the equality of man; and I hope for happiness beyond this life. I believe in the equality of man; and I believe that religious duties consist of doing justice, loving mercy, and endeavoring to make our fellow creatures happy.

But, lest it be supposed that I believe many other things in addition to these, I shall, in the progress of this work, declare the things I do not believe, and my reasons for not believing them.

I do not believe in the creed professed by the Jewish church, by the Roman church, by the Greek church, by the Turkish church, by the Protestant church, nor by any church that I know of. My mind is my own church.

Castigated and condemned for *The Age of Reason* in his later years, Paine attained great stature in American thought by the twentieth century. In 1945, he was elected to the American Hall of Fame, and in recent years, monuments to him have been erected at Morristown, New Jersey, Paris, France, and Thetford, England. In 1884, the Thomas Paine National Historical Association was organized in his memory. Its Memorial Hall in New Rochelle, along with the nearby Paine cottage, are open to the public.

The best book on Paine's religious beliefs is Ira M. Thompson, Jr.'s *Religious Beliefs of Thomas Paine* (154); this is a well-documented study, with an excellent bibliography. Other important books on Paine are as follows:

Biographies: 50, 56, 57, 58, 66, 74, 81, 95, 132, 137, 144, 145, 158, 164, 166, and 169.

Collections of Paine's Works: 71, 75, 80, 85, 112, 118, 159, and 164.
Books with a chapter on Paine: 32, 37, 63, and 116.
Books of a general nature: 9, 21, 27, 28, 32, and 33.
Fictionalized epic novel: 111.

The most active of the militant Deists of this period was Elihu Palmer (1764-1806). He was born and raised in Connecticut, attended Dartmouth College (graduating in 1787), and entered the ministry at Pittsfield, Massachusetts. After a few months, he received a call from Newton, Long Island, but lasted only six months because of his liberal sentiments. He then went to Philadelphia, where he became a Baptist minister, but again he was dismissed for his liberal views. Palmer next joined the Universal Society, which had been founded by John Fitch (the inventor of the steamboat). In one of his addresses to the society, he so forcefully denied the divinity of Jesus that the Episcopal bishop, upon hearing of his sermon, used his influence to deprive the group of a meeting place. As a result, the Universal Society disbanded and Palmer was forced to flee Philadelphia. He then studied law under the direction of his brother in western Pennsylvania and was admitted to the bar at Philadelphia in 1793. Three months later, a yellow fever epidemic took the life of his wife and left him permanently blind. With law no longer possible for him, he became a freelance Deistic preacher. He went to Augusta, Georgia, for a year and finally came to New York City, which was to be the center of his Deistic activities for the remainder of his life. Palmer founded a Deistical Society in New York during the winter of 1796-1797, lecturing before this group for the next few years. Palmer occasionally lectured to sister organizations formed in Philadelphia and Baltimore, as well as to the Society of the Ancient Druids, a Deistical group at Newburgh, New York. During this time, Palmer also wrote for two magazines, *The Temple of Reason* (152) and *Prospect: or View of the Moral World* (136). His championing of Deism only brought him poverty and opposition.

The most complete statement of Palmer's thinking is found in his *Principles of Nature* (130), the first edition of which was published in New York in 1801 or 1802. Although it was reprinted several times, including a British edition, the book is extremely rare today.

The following quotation from *Principles of Nature* fairly summarizes Palmer's beliefs:

Deism declares to intelligent man the existence of one perfect God, Creator and Preserver of the Universe; that the laws by which he governs the world are like himself immutable, and, of course, that violations of these laws, or miraculous interference in the movements of nature, must be necessarily excluded from the grand system of universal existence; that the Creator is entitled to the adoration of every intellectual agent throughout the regions of infinite space; and that he alone is entitled to it, having no co-partners who have a right to share with him the homage of the intelligent world. Deism also declares that the practice of a pure, natural and uncorrupted virtue, is the essential duty, and constitutes the highest dignity of man; that the powers of man are competent to all the great purposes of human existence; that science, virtue, and happiness, are the great objects which ought to awake the mental energies, and draw forth the moral affections of the human race.

These are the outlines of pure Deism, which Christian superstition dreadfully abhors and whose votaries she would willingly consign to endless torture. But it is built upon a substantial foundation, and will triumphantly diffuse happiness among the nations of the earth, for ages after Christian superstition and fanaticism have ceased to spread desolation and carnage through the fair creation of God.

No biography of Palmer has ever been written. An article on Palmer appears in the *Dictionary of American Biography* (79), and a short sketch in *Posthumous Pieces, Elihu Palmer* (131). Further information may be found in references 21, 22, 27, and 28.

Two literary figures of this period, Joel Barlow (1754-1812) and Philip Freneau (1752-1832), were Deists. Barlow was also involved in the political history of the early federal government. Biographies and articles describing Barlow's and Freneau's religious views include *A Yankee's Odyssey, The Life of Joel Barlow* (168), *Joel Barlow* (88), "Joel Barlow, Enlightened Religionist" in the *Journal of the History of Ideas* (59), *Philip Freneau and the Cosmic Enigma* (47), *Philip Freneau, Champion of Democracy* (52), and *Poems of Freneau* (70).

* * *

In the late eighteenth century, a number of societies were formed to further disseminate Deism. In 1790, John Fitch (1743-1798) founded the Universal Society in Philadelphia. Originally a Methodist, Fitch had become disillusioned with Methodism when his fellow Methodists in Trenton, New Jersey, censured him for working on Sundays to supply the American troops with arms during the Revolutionary War, and he later became an avowed disbeliever. (For biographies of Fitch, see references 62 and 163.) As noted earlier, as a result of Elihu Palmer's controversial sermons, the Universal Society disbanded around 1791.

Another society established during this period was Palmer's Deistical Society (1796-1797). Palmer lectured each Sunday evening to his group. Palmer's statement of principles for the society proclaimed that one supreme Deity exists, that man is possessed of moral and intellectual faculties sufficient for the improvement of his nature and the acquisition of his happiness, that the religion of nature is the only universal religion, and that there is a necessity for civil and religious liberty. Every member was to deem it his duty to promote the cause of nature and moral truth, in opposition to all schemes of superstition and fanaticism which claimed divine origin.

The society was not successful, partly because it could not attract the wealthier people in the community. It gained new life with the weekly publication entitled *The Temple of Reason* (152) to report on their activities. The society was weakened when it began to mix in the politics of the city. In 1804, Palmer tried to raise funds to erect a Temple of Nature in New York City, no doubt because his group was frequently forced to change meeting places. Nothing came of this attempt, and when Palmer died in 1806, the Deistical Society languished.

In the meantime, the Deists formed a group called the Theophilanthropists in Philadelphia. Palmer also lectured to this group. The Theophilanthropists attempted to erect a permanent building for their lectures but were unsuccessful, and eventually the group disbanded.

Another society, the Society of the Ancient Druids, was organized in Newburgh, New York, and developed from the Masonic Lodge which had been formed in Newburgh in 1788. The Newburgh Druids were considered more radical than the Deists of New York or Philadelphia. They too came under the influence of Palmer, who lectured before the group and received an annual salary. The Druids published a weekly infidel paper called *The Mirror* (120), and reprinted and circulated Paine's *The Age of Reason* (125), Tindal's *Christianity as Old as the Creation* (155), and similar books. After 1800, the Druids declined and were not heard of again after 1804.

Baltimore's Deistic organization was called the Theophilanthropic Society.

Deistic societies flourished from 1794 until Palmer's death in 1806, when organized Deism began to go into a decline. Early in 1810, some of the old guard began to publish *The Theophilanthropist* (153), but it was even less successful than *The Temple of Reason* (152).

For additional information on Deistic organizations, see references 21, 27, and 138.

* * *

A very important Deistic work that appeared in the United States during this period was *The Ruins, or Meditations on the Revolutions of Empires and the Laws of Nature* (160) by Constantin François

Chassebouf, Count de Volney, of France. A translation of this work was started by Thomas Jefferson and completed by Joel Barlow. In this oversimplified study of comparative religions, Volney pointed out that all religions were means by which designing men obtained power and wealth. The book was intended as a companion volume to Paine's *The Age of Reason.* Volney's two-year stay in the United States helped promote the popularity of *The Ruins.*

Another freethought book that appeared at the very end of this period was *The Grounds of Christianity Examined* (83) by George Bethune English (1787-1828). After failing as a minister, English wrote this 182-page volume in which he carefully analyzed the Old and New Testament, concluding that they were not only contradictory, but also not divine. His book stirred up some controversy in its time. A biographical sketch of English appears in the *Dictionary of American Biography* (79).

* * *

As mentioned earlier, the first freethought book published in the United States was Ethan Allen's *Reason the Only Oracle of Man* (51), published in 1784. However, the publishers of this volume did not publish other freethought books and therefore could not really be called freethought publishers.

One of the earliest freethought best sellers in the United States was Paine's *The Age of Reason* (125). The first U.S. edition was published in 1795. Of all its early publishers, only one could be called a freethought publisher in the sense that he issued several freethought books. This was John Fellows, a personal friend of Thomas Paine. The firm soon became T. & J. Swords for J. Fellows.

The early freethought publishers in the United States made up their lists of books from the classics of freethought published abroad. Included were the English translations of D'Holbach's *The System of Nature* (100) and *Good Sense* (99) (sometimes called *Common Sense*), Voltaire's *Philosophical Dictionary* (161), Volney's *Ruins of Empires* (160), and some of Diderot's works. Later, early American freethought books, such as Elihu Palmer's *Principles of Nature* (130), would be added to Paine's various works and the European classics to make up the entire list.

The first U.S. publishers who had a freethought list of sorts seems to have been the Columbian Press (New York, circa 1795), but most began publishing in the 1825-1830 period. They will therefore be covered in Chapter 2.

The following references provide additional information on the Deistic movement in the United States: 48, 53, 76, 94, 123, 134, 138, 142, 147, 150, and 151.

* * *

During the Deistic period, liberalizing tendencies at work within the church gave rise to the development of Unitarianism and Univversalism. American Unitarianism developed out of New England Congregationalism. The latitudinarian movement within the Anglican church also hastened the growth of Unitarianism and Universalism, as well as of Deism. Arminianism, which got its name from Jacobus Arminius (1560-1609), the Dutch remonstrant, was a reaction against Calvinism. Arminian ministers who did much to liberalize the church during this period were Ebenezer Gay (1696-1787), Charles Chauncy (1705-1787), Jonathan Mayhew (1720-1766), William Bentley (1759-1819), and James Freeman (1759-1835). Freeman's church, Kings Chapel in Boston (Anglican), became the first Unitarian church in the United States.

John Murray (1741-1815) established the first Universalist church in America. Others who assisted in the growth of Universalism included Dr. George de Benneville (1703-1793) and Elhanan Winchester (1751-1797). Two other very important figures in the history of Unitarianism and Universalism were William Ellery Channing (1780-1842) and Hosea Ballou (1771-1852). Since Channing and Ballou belong to the first half of the nineteenth century, they will be discussed in Chapter 2.

The growth of Unitarianism and Universalism are discussed in references 9, 16, 21, 27, 37, 46, 67, 84, 142, 165, and 171. An excellent bibliography on Unitarianism and Universalism is provided in *A Critical Bibliography of Religion in America* (10).

BIBLIOGRAPHY

47. Adkins, Nelson F. *Philip Freneau and the Cosmic Enigma. The Religious and Philosophical Speculations of an American Poet.* New York: New York University Press, 1949.

48. Ahlstrom, Sidney E. *A Religious History of the American People.* New Haven: Yale University Press, 1972, 2 vols.

49. Aldridge, Alfred Owen. *Benjamin Franklin and Nature's God.* Durham, N.C.: Duke University Press, 1967. The best book on Franklin's religion.

50. Aldridge, Alfred Owen. *Man of Reason: The Life of Thomas Paine.* Philadelphia: J. B. Lippincott, 1959.

51. Allen, Ethan. *Reason the Only Oracle of Man.* Bennington, Vt.: Haswell & Russell, 1784. An abridged edition published by G. W. and A. J. Matsell, Philadelphia, 1836 and by J. P. Mendum, Boston, 1854. A facsimile reprint of the original issued by Scholars' Facsimiles & Reprints, New York, 1940.

52. Axelrod, Jacob. *Philip Freneau, Champion of Democracy.* Austin: University of Texas Press, 1967.

53. Bates, Ernest Sutherland. *American Faith.* New York: W. W. Norton, 1940. Chapter 20, entitled "The Rise of Deism," is an excellent summary of the extent of the Deistic movement in the United States.

54. Bayle, Pierre. *Philosophical Commentary on the Words of Jesus "Compel Them to Come in That My House May Be Full."* First English translation was London: J. Darby, 1708, 2 vols.

55. Berlin, Isaiah. *The Age of Enlightenment: The 18th Century Philosophers.* New York: New American Library, 1956.

56. Berthold, S. M. *Thomas Paine: America's First Liberal.* Boston: Meader Publishing Co., 1938.

57. Best, Mary A. *Thomas Paine, Prophet and Martyr of Democracy.* New York: Harcourt, Brace & Co., 1927.

58. Blanchard, Calvin. *The Life of Thomas Paine.* New York: Calvin Blanchard, 1860.

59. Blau, Joseph. "Joel Barlow, Enlightened Religionist."*Journal of the History of Ideas* 10 (1949):430-444.

60. Blount, Charles. *Oracles of Reason.* London: no publisher, "1693" [i.e., 1695].

61. Boller, Paul F., Jr. *George Washington and Religion.* Dallas: Southern Methodist University Press, 1963.

62. Boyd, Thomas. *Poor John Fitch: Inventor of the Steamboat.* New York, G. P. Putnam's Sons, 1935.

63. Bradford, Gamaliel. *Damaged Souls.* Boston: Houghton Mifflin Co., 1923.

64. Brinton, Clarence Crane. *The Portable Age of Reason Reader.* New York: Viking Press, 1956.

65. Butler, Joseph. *The Analogy of Religion, Natural and Revealed, to the Constitution and Course of Nature.* London: James, John & Paul Knapton, 1737.

66. Carlile, Richard. *The Life of Thomas Paine.* London: R. Carlile, 1819.

67. Cheetham, Henry H. *Unitarianism and Universalism: An Illustrated History.* Boston: Beacon Press, 1962.

68. Chubb, Thomas. *Discourse Concerning Reason.* London: T. Cox, 1731.

69. Chubb, Thomas. *The True Gospel of Jesus Asserted.* London: T. Cox, 1738.

70. Clark, Harry Hayden, ed. *Poems of Freneau.* New York: Hafner Publishing Co., 1929.

71. Clark, Harry Hayden. *Thomas Paine: Representative Selections.* New York: American Book Co., 1944. Contains a good bibliography.

72. Collins, Anthony. *A Discourse of Freethinking.* London: no publisher, 1713.

73. Collins, Anthony. *Discourse on the Grounds and Reasons of the Christian Religion.* No place: no publisher, 1724.

74. Conway, Moncure Daniel. *The Life of Thomas Paine.* New York: G. P. Putnam's Sons, 1892, 2 vols.

75. Conway, Moncure Daniel, ed. *The Writings of Thomas Paine.* New York: G. P. Putnam's Sons, 1894-1896, 4 vols.

76. Cousins, Norman, ed. *"In God We Trust," The Religious Beliefs and Ideas of the American Founding Fathers.* New York: Harper & Brothers, 1958. Contains the letters of Franklin, Washington, Jefferson, Adams, and Paine in which they express their religious views.

77. Descartes, Rene. *Discourse on Method.* Leiden: Jan Maire, 1637.

78. Dewey, John, ed. *The Living Thoughts of Thomas Jefferson.* New York: Longmans Green & Co., 1940.

79. *Dictionary of American Biography.* Edited by Allen Johnson and Dumas Malone. New York: Charles Scribner's Sons, 1928-1936.

80. Dos Passos, John, ed. *The Living Thoughts of Thomas Paine.* New York: Longmans Green & Co., 1940.

81. Edwards, Samuel. *Rebel! A Biography of Thomas Paine.* New York: Praeger Publishers, 1974.

82. *Encyclopedie.* Paris: no publisher, 1751-1780, 36 vols.

83. English, George Bethune. *The Grounds of Christianity Examined.* Boston: no publisher, 1813.

84. Ferm, Vergilius, ed. *The American Church of the Protestant Heritage.* New York: Philosophical Library, 1953.

85. Foner, Philip, ed. *The Complete Writings of Thomas Paine.* New York: Citadel Press, 1945, 2 vols.

86. Foote, Henry Wilder. *The Religion of Thomas Jefferson.* Boston: Beacon Press, 1960.

87. Foote, Henry Wilder. *Thomas Jefferson: Champion of Religious Freedom, Advocate of Christian Morals.* Boston: Beacon Press, 1947.

88. Ford, Arthur L. *Joel Barlow.* New York: Twayne Publishers, 1971.

89. Franklin, Benjamin. *Articles of Belief and Acts of Religion.* Philadelphia: Published by the Author, 1728. Included in *The Development of American Philosophy* (reference 28) and in *Papers of Benjamin Franklin,* New Haven: Yale University Press, 1959.

90. Franklin, Benjamin. *Autobiography.* Paris and London: various publishers, 1771-1789. Published in sections, often out of chronological sequence.

91. Franklin, Benjamin. *Dissertation on Liberty and Necessity, Pleasure and Pain.* London: no publisher, 1725.

92. Gay, Peter. *The Age of Enlightenment.* New York: Time, Inc., 1966.

93. Hall, Henry. *Ethan Allen.* New York: D. Appleton & Co., 1892.

94. Hallgren, Mauritz A. *Landscape of Freedom, The Story of American Liberty and Bigotry.* New York: Howell, Soskin & Co., 1941.

95. Hawke, David. *Paine.* New York: Harper & Row, 1974. Perhaps the best biography of Paine.

96. Hazard, Paul. *European Thought in the Eighteenth Century from Montesquieu to Lessing.* New Haven: Yale University Press, 1954.

97. Healy, Robert M. *Jefferson on Religion in Public Education.* New Haven: Yale University Press, 1962. One of the best books on Jefferson's religion.

98. Herbert, Edward, First Baron of Cherbury. *Religion of the Gentiles With the Causes of Their Errors.* Amsterdam: Typis Blaevorum, 1663. First English translation was London: John Nutt, 1705.

99. Holbach, Paul Henry Thiry, Baron D'. *Good Sense.* "London:" [Amsterdam: M. M. Rey], 1772. Often mistakenly confused with *My Testament* by Meslier, to whom it is often attributed in error.

100. Holbach, Paul Henry Thiry, Baron D'. *The System of Nature.* "London:" [Amsterdam: M. M. Rey], 1770. Often called "The Bible of Atheism."

101. Holbrook, Stewart H. *Ethan Allen.* New York: Macmillan Co., 1944.

102. Hume, David. *Dialogues Concerning Natural Religion.* London: no publisher, 1779.

103. Hume, David. *Philosophical Essays Concerning Human Understanding.* London: A. Millar, 1748.

104. Hume, David. *Essay on Miracles.* First published as Chapter X of no. 103 above.

105. Hume, David. *Treatise on Human Nature.* London: vols. 1 & 2

published by John Noon, 1779; vol. 3 published by Thomas Longman.

106. Jefferson, Thomas. *The Jefferson Bible: Being the Life and Morals of Jesus of Nazareth, Extracted Textually From the Gospels of Matthew, Mark, Luke and John.* St. Louis: Thompson Publishing Co., n.d. [1902]. Not published until long after Jefferson died.

107. Koch, Adrienne. *The Philosophy of Thomas Jefferson.* New York: Columbia University Press, 1943.

108. la Mettrie, Julian de. *Man A Machine.* Leiden: Elie Luzac, Jr., 1748. First English translation was London: W. Owen, 1749.

109. Law, William. *The Case of Reason, or Natural Religion Fairly Stated.* London: W. Innys, 1731.

110. Lehman, Karl. *Thomas Jefferson: American Humanist.* New York: Macmillan Co., 1947.

111. Levin, Benjamin H. *To Spit Against the Wind.* New York: Citadel Press, 1970. A fictionalized epic novel about Thomas Paine.

112. Lewis, Joseph. *Inspiration and Wisdom from the Writings of Thomas Paine.* New York: Freethought Press Assoc., 1954.

113. Locke, John. *Essay Concerning Human Understanding.* London: Elizabeth Holt for Thomas Basset, 1690.

114. Locke, John. *Letters on Toleration.* London: various publishers, 1689-1692.

115. Locke, John. *Reasonableness of Christianity.* London: Printed for Awnsham and John Churchil, 1695.

116. McConnell, Francis J. *Evangelicals, Revolutionists, and Idealists.* New York: Abingdon-Cokesbury Press, 1942. Has a chapter on Thomas Paine.

117. Manuel, Frank E., ed. *The Enlightenment.* Englewood Cliffs, N.J.: Prentice-Hall, 1965.

118. Mendum, J. P., ed. *Theological Works of Thomas Paine.* Boston: J. P. Mendum, 1858.

119. Merrill, Walter McIntosh. *From Statesman to Philosopher, A Study of Bolingbroke's Deism.* New York: Philosophical Library, 1949.

120. *Mirror, The,* a weekly infidel periodical published by the Society of the Ancient Druids of Newburgh, N.Y., 1798-1799.

121. Mossner, Ernest Campbell. *Bishop Butler and the Age of Reason: A Study in the History of Thought.* New York: Macmillan Co.., 1936.

122. Newton, Isaac. *Principia Mathematica.* London: Joseph Streater for the Royal Society, 1687.

123. Olmstead, Clifton E. *History of Religion in the United States.* Englewood Cliffs, N.J.: Prentice-Hall, 1960.

124. Orr, John. *English Deism: Its Roots and Its Fruits.* Grand

Rapids, Mich.: W. B. Eerdmans Publishing Co., 1934.

125. Paine, Thomas. *The Age of Reason.* Part I, Paris: Barrois, Sr., 1794; Part II, London: H. D. Symonds, 1795. Many editions have since been published, although the early printing history is rather confused.

126. Paine, Thomas. *Common Sense.* Philadelphia: R. Bell, 1776.

127. Paine, Thomas. *The Crisis.* Various places: various publishers, 1776. Originally issued in separate parts.

128. Paley, William. *Natural Theology.* London: R. Faulder, 1802.

129. Paley, William. *View of the Evidences of Christianity.* London: R. Faulder, 1794.

130. Palmer, Elihu. *Principles of Nature.* New York: Printed for the Author, n.d. [1801 or 1802]. Several subsequent editions, including a British one published in London by R. Carlile.

131. Palmer, Elihu. *Posthumous Pieces, Elihu Palmer. Being three chapters of an unfinished work intended to have been entitled "The Political World." To which are prefixed a Memoir of Mr. Palmer by his friend Mr. John Fellows of New York, and Mr. Palmer's "Principles of the Deistical Society of the State of New York."* London: R. Carlile, 1826. No American edition ever published.

132. Pearson, Hesketh. *Tom Paine, Friend of Mankind.* New York: Harper & Brothers, 1937.

133. Pell, John. *Ethan Allen.* Boston: Houghton Mifflin Co., 1929.

134. Persons, Stow. *American Minds, A History of Ideas.* New York: Henry Holt & Co., 1958.

135. Pike, E. Royston. *Slayers of Superstition: A Popular Account of the Leading Personalities of the Deist Movement.* London: Watts & Co., 1931. One of the best brief accounts.

136. *Prospect, or View of the Moral World,* a weekly Deistic magazine published in New York by Elihu Palmer from December 10, 1803, to March 30, 1805.

137. Remsberg, John E. *Thomas Paine, Apostle of Religious and Political Liberty.* Boston: J. P. Mendum, 1880.

138. Riley, Isaac Woodbridge. "Early Freethinking Societies in America." *Harvard Theological Review* 11 (1918):247-284.

139. Rousseau, Jean-Jacques. *Emile.* Amsterdam: J Néaulme, 1762.

140. Rousseau, Jean-Jacques. *Social Contract.* Amsterdam: [M. M. Rey], 1762.

141. Russell, Phillips. *Jefferson: Champion of the Free Mind.* New York: Dodd, Mead & Co., 1956.

142. Savelle, Max. *Seeds of Liberty: The Genesis of the American Mind.* New York: Alfred A. Knopf, 1948. An excellent discussion of how Deism developed in the United States prior to the American Revolution.

143. Schantz, B. T. "Ethan Allen's Religious Ideas." *Journal of Religion* 18 (1938):183-217.

144. Sedgwick, Ellery. *Thomas Paine.* Boston: Small, Maynard, 1899.

145. Smith, Frank. *Thomas Paine, Liberator.* New York: Frederick A. Stokes, 1938.

146. Snyder, Louis L. *The Age of Reason.* New York: D. Van Nostrand Co., 1955. An excellent brief account of the Age of Reason, with selected readings from some of the great books of the period.

147. Sonne, Niels Henry. *Liberal Kentucky, 1780-1828.* New York: Columbia University Press, 1939. Tells about the spread of Deism in Kentucky.

148. Stifler, James Madison. *The Religion of Benjamin Franklin.* New York: D. Appleton & Co., 1925.

149. Swancara, Frank. *Thomas Jefferson vs. Religious Oppression.* New York: University Books, 1969.

150. Sweet, William Warren. *Religion in Colonial America.* New York: Charles Scribner's Sons, 1942.

151. Sweet, William Warren. *Religion in the Development of American Culture, 1765-1840.* New York: Charles Scribner's Sons, 1942.

152. *Temple of Reason, The,* a weekly Deistic magazine published in New York from November 8, 1800, to February 7, 1801, and then in Philadelphia from April 22, 1801, to February 19, 1803.

153. *Theophilanthropist, The,* a weekly Deistic magazine published in New York intermittently during 1810-1811. Nine issues published.

154. Thompson, Ira M., Jr. *The Religious Beliefs of Thomas Paine.* New York: Vantage Press, 1965.

155. Tindal, Matthew. *Christinaity as Old as the Creation.* London: no publisher, 1730.

156. Toland, John. *Christianity Not Mysterious.* London: S. Buckley, 1696.

157. Torrey, Norman L. *Voltaire and the English Deists.* New Haven: Yale University Press, 1930.

158. Vale, Gilbert. *The Life of Thomas Paine.* New York: Published by the Author, 1841.

159. Van der Weyde, William M., ed. *The Life and Works of Thom-*

as Paine. New Rochelle, N.Y.: Thomas Paine Historical Assoc., 1925, 10 vols. Life is by Van der Weyde.

160. Volney, Count Constantin François Chasseboeuf de. *The Ruins, or Meditations on the Revolutions of Empires and the Laws of Nature.* Paris: no publisher, 1791.

161. Voltaire, François Marie Arouet de. *Philosophical Dictionary.* "London:" [Geneva:] no publisher, 1764.

162. Waring, E. Graham, ed. *Deism and Natural Religion, A Source Book.* New York: Frederick Ungar Publishing Co., 1967.

163. Westcott, Thompson. *The Life of John Fitch, Inventor of the Steamboat.* Philadelphia: J. B. Lippincott, 1878.

164. Wheeler, Daniel E., ed. *The Life and Writings of Thomas Paine.* New York: V. Park & Co., 1915, 10 vols.

165. Wilbur, Earl Morse. *Our Unitarian Heritage.* Boston: Beacon Press, 1925.

166. Williamson, Audrey. *Thomas Paine: His Life, Work and Times.* New York: St. Martin's Press, 1973.

167. Wollaston, William. *The Religion of Nature Delineated.* London: J. Knapton, 1722.

168. Woodress, James. *A Yankee's Odyssey, The Life of Joel Barlow.* Philadelphia: J.B. Lipincott Co., 1958.

169. Woodward, William E. *Thomas Paine, America's Godfather.* New York: E.P. Dutton & Co., 1945.

170. Woolston, Thomas. *Discourses on the Miracles of Our Savior.* London: no publisher, 1727-1730. Issued in six parts.

171. Wright, Conrad. *The Beginnings of Unitarianism in America.* Boston: Beacon Press, 1955. One of the best books on the subject.

2.

★★★★★★★★★

Popular Freethought

Following the death of Thomas Paine and Elihu Palmer, freethought activity in America almost completely ceased; it was not revived until the mid- and late 1820s. Many of the leading freethought exponents now included people who had come to America from Great Britain.

By far the most complete book on freethought in the 1825-1860 period is *Popular Freethought in America, 1825-1850* (29) by Albert Post. It is indispensable to the student of freethought in America, giving a fully documented account of the leading personalities, organizations, and publications of the time.

The leading personalities during this period were Frances Wright, Robert Dale Owen, George Houston, Thomas Hertell, Benjamin Offen, Abner Kneeland, Gilbert Vale, and Ernestine Rose.

Frances Wright (1795-1852) was of Scottish parentage and was born in Dundee, Scotland. She lost both parents when she was only two years old, and she was raised and educated by relatives. Despite her wealthy, upper class background, Wright became associated with many of the radical movements of her time. Having already made a visit to America in 1818, she returned in 1824 to attempt to establish a colony at Nashoba, Tennessee, as a home for freed slaves. When this colony failed, she became associated with Robert Dale Owen (1801-1877) in the publication of the freethought magazine *The New Harmony Gazette* (186), which was the organ of the Robert Owen colony at New Harmony, Indiana. This colony also eventually failed, and the magazine moved to New York City, changing its name to *The Free Enquirer* (186).

Wright was a brilliant speaker of extraordinary ability. In the late 1820s and early 1830s, she lectured in many of the cities of the

United States. The themes of her lectures included "Chartered Mon-
opolies," "Southern Slavery," "Existing Evils and Their Remedy,"
"Religion," "Morals," and "Free Inquiry." Her lectures were published
in a book entitled *Course of Popular Lectures* (244). After her marriage to William Phiquepal D'Arusmont, she became less active in freethought circles. She retired to Cincinnati where she lived during the
last sixteen years of her life. A number of biographies of Frances
Wright have been written, including those in references 202, 219,
229, and 236.

Robert Dale Owen was born in Glasgow, Scotland in 1801 and
was educated in Switzerland. He came to America in 1825 with his
father, Robert Owen, to assist in the establishment of what was to
be a model utopian community at New Harmony, Indiana. Dale Owen
became the editor of *The New Harmony Gazette* (186), which later
became *The Free Enquirer* (186). In addition to his activities as editor,
Owen lectured frequently on freethought, also establishing an exten-
sive and profitable freethought bookstore in New York. In 1832, Owen
went to Europe, leaving *The Free Enquirer* under the supervision of
Amos Gilbert. When Owen returned to America, he went to Indiana,
where he began a political career that took him to Congress and then
to Naples as a government minister. Later in life, Owen was converted
to Spiritualism. There is an excellent biography of Owen, called *Robert
Dale Owen, A Biography* (203), by Richard William Leopold, as well
as an autobiography entitled *Twenty-seven Years of Autobiography,
Threading My Way* (217).

George Houston (? -1840) came to the more congenial atmos-
phere of America around 1820, after having served a two-year sen-
tence for publishing "blasphemous" literature in Great Britain. In 1827,
he established his weekly freethought journal *The Correspondent*
(184), which ran for more than two years. Houston also engaged in
some freethought lecturing.

One of the most distinguished and respected liberals of this period
was Thomas Hertell (1771-1849), a member of the State Assembly
of New York and for many years a judge in New York City. As a member of the Assembly, he spoke out forcibly for his liberal views. These
views are printed in Hertell's *The Spirit of Truth: Being an Exposition
of Infidelity or Religious Belief* (193).

Benjamin Offen (1772-1848), a self-educated English shoemaker,
came to America in 1824. After spending one year at West Point, he
went to New York City, where he was quite active in freethought affairs
until his death. An excellent speaker, he lectured regularly before the

freethought organizations in New York. For his religious views, see *A Legacy to the Friends of Free Discussion . . .* z)215). There is a biographical sketch of Offen in *The World's Sages, Infidels and Thinkers* (6).

Abner Kneeland (1774-1844) was born in Gardner, Massachusetts, of English and Irish ancestry. Early in life he worked at the carpenter's trade, after which he became a Baptist preacher. Because of his liberal thinking, he left the Baptist church and became a Universalist minister. In 1825, he moved to New York City, shortly thereafter renouncing the Christian religion altogether and becoming a freethought lecturer. In 1829, he delivered a series of freethought lectures which were published under the title *A Review of the Evidences of Christianity* (199). These passed through several editions. In 1831, Kneeland accepted a position as lecturer to the Free Enquirers of Boston. He established *The Boston Investigator* (177), a weekly that became one of the longest lived (1831-1904) freethought publications in the United States.

In 1833, Kneeland was arrested and indicted on a charge of blasphemy (under a 1782 law) for saying that he did not believe in the God of the Universalists. The trial began in January 1834, and after three more trials lasting four years, he was found guilty and sentenced to sixty days in jail. In 1839, Kneeland moved to Iowa, where he failed in his attempt to set up a freethought community.

No biography of Kneeland has ever been written, but a biographical sketch appears in the *Dictionary of American Biography* (79). Biographical sketches are also included in references 6, 30, and 46. For an account of his blasphemy trial, see Commager's article in *The New England Quarterly* (182).

Gilbert Vale (1788-1866) was born in London and educated for the church. He abandoned that course and became a freethinker. He came to New York in 1829 where he taught surveying, navigation, and mathematics for a livelihood. During the 1830s and 1840s, he was quite active in spreading freethought, both by lecturing and by publishing a freethought paper named *The Beacon* (175). Vale also wrote a biography of Thomas Paine (158) and was instrumental in raising the funds to build a monument to Paine on his farm in New Rochelle, New York, in 1839. No biography of Vale has been written, but there is a biographical sketch in *Appleton's Cyclopedia of American Biography* (174).

Ernestine Louise Siismondi Potowski Rose (1810-1892) was born in Poland of Jewish parents. Early in life she rebelled against orthodox Judaism; she traveled throughout Europe and eventually settled in England. After her marriage to William E. Rose, she came to New York in 1836, which remained her home until her return to England in 1874. During her stay in America, she was very active in the reform movements of the time, particularly women's rights, abolition, free schools, and freethought. Despite her foreign accent, she was a brilliant lecturer for the causes she favored. An excellent biography of Rose is *Ernestine L. Rose and the Battle for Human Rights* (231) by Yuri Suhl. There is also a short article about her in the *Dictionary of American Biography* (79). Her ability as a speaker is discussed in reference 179.

Thomas Cooper (1759-1839) was not directly connected with the freethought movement, but made some definite contributions to freethought. After he came to America from England, Cooper was professor of chemistry at Dickinson College, the University of Pennsylvania, and finally at the University of South Carolina, of which he later became president. Cooper, a materialist and skeptic, generally found himself in the midst of controversy for his unorthodox views. He was a prolific writer, his many books expressing his anti-clerical and materialistic ideas. A biography entitled *The Public Life of Thomas Cooper, 1783-1839* (208) has been written by Dumas Malone, and a biographical sketch appears in the *Dictionary of American Biography* (79). See also references 1 and 38.

One of the heroes of freethinkers of this period was Stephen Girard (1750-1831). Born in France, he settled in Philadelphia, where he made a fortune in shipping. Although Girard was never directly associated with freethought, his sympathy for the movement is suggested by the names he gave his ships, such as the *Voltaire, Rousseau,* and *Helvetius.* Girard willed about $6 million for the endowment of a college for orphans in Philadelphia, where "no ecclesiastic missionary, or minister of any sect whatever shall ever hold or exercise any station of duty whatever in the said college." Two biographies of Girard are *Lonely Midas, the Story of Stephen Girard* (239) by Harry Emerson Wildes and *Life and Character of Stephen Girard* (197) by H. A. Ingram.

Abraham Lincoln has been claimed by freethinkers as one of their own on the basis that he never joined a church and was somewhat unorthodox in his religious thinking. The best book on Lincoln's religious beliefs is *The Religion of Abraham Lincoln* (241) by William J. Wolf. See also references 173 and 180.

* * *

The first Thomas Paine birthday celebration, held on January 29, 1825, marks the revival of organized freethought in the United States.

These admirers of Paine formed the Free Press Association on January 29, 1827. In addition to assisting the freethought magazine *The Correspondent* (184), the association inaugurated weekly lectures, which became quite popular. The Free Press Association seems to have existed for only a little over two years.

Another freethought organization of this period was the Free Enquirers, started in February 1828 to provide activities for the upper section of New York City. The most long-lived freethought organization in New York City, however, was the Moral Philanthropists, which lasted from 1829 to 1839. In 1842, a Society of Free Enquirers was organized as a successor to this group. George Houston, Frances Wright, Robert Dale Owen, and Benjamin Offen lectured more or less regularly before these and other freethought organizations.

In Boston, the First Society of Free Enquirers was organized in 1830. Abner Kneeland lectured regularly before this group. The Society continued until 1840, at which time the Boston Discussion Society was organized; the Boston Society continued until 1845.

Although the most vigorous freethought societies were in New York and Boston, societies were also organized in Rochester, New York; Paterson, New Jersey; Pittsburgh, Pennsylvania; St. Louis, Missouri, and many smaller cities.

By the 1830s, many freethinkers sought to establish a national organization. In August 1836, a convention was held at Saratoga Springs, New York, at which Abner Kneeland and Benjamin Offen urged a national organization. A constitution was prepared and adopted, with the new organization taking the name The United Moral and Philosophical Society for the Diffusion of Useful Knowledge. Isaac S. Smith of Buffalo was elected president, and Oliver White, John Wood, and Thomas Thompson were elected vice-president, secretary, and treasurer, respectively. The United Moral and Philosophical Society lasted from 1836 to 1841, with annual conventions held in New York City (except in 1839, when the convention was held in Rochester, New York). Most of the local organizations belonging to this national society came from New York and Ohio, with Illinois, Pennsylvania, Michigan, Mississippi, and Georgia also being represented. The presidents of the national organization during this time were Isaac Smith, Thomas Hertell, Ransom Cook, and Oliver White; most of the work of the organization, however, fell to the secretary, Gilbert Vale.

The next attempt at national organization was made at a convention held in New York City in 1845. The meeting was attended by 196 delegates, more than half of whom were from New York. Other states represented were Pennsylvania, New Jersey, Indiana, Ohio,

Illinois, Kentucky, Alabama, and South Carolina. Thomas Hertell, Benjamin Offen, Ernestine Rose, Gilbert Vale, and Horace Seaver were in attendance. After much disagreement, the name The Infidel Society for the Promotion of Mental Liberty was chosen for the organization. Hertell was chosen president and James M. Beckett recording secretary. The proceedings of this convention were published as *Meteor of Light, Containing the Minutes of the Proceedings of the Infidel Convention held in the City of New York, May 4th, 5th and 6th, 1845* (210).

The first anniversary convention of the Infidel Society was held in New York City, with only forty delegates in attendance. Hertell was reelected president. The third (and probably the last) convention was held in New York City in May 1847, with still fewer delegates attending.

The next freethought convention which was national in scope was the Hartford Bible Convention held in 1854 for the purpose of "freely and fully canvassing the origin, authority and influence of the Jewish and Christian scriptures." The meeting is fully reported in *Proceedings of the Hartford Bible Convention* (190), edited by Andrew J. Graham.

In September 1857, yet another attempt at national organization was made when the Infidel Association of the United States met in Philadelphia in response to a call by Robert Wallin in *The Boston Investigator* (177). This meeting is also reported in the publication *Minutes of the Infidel Convention Held in the City of Philadelphia, Sept. 7th and 8th, 1857* (211).

It was during this period that Robert Owen (1771-1858), the father of Robert Dale Owen, tried to start a cooperative colony at New Harmony, Indiana. Owen, who had amassed a fortune in textile manufacturing, purchased the Rappite Community in Indiana, where he hoped to bring about the social, economic, and religious reforms he espoused. Almost a thousand people from all walks of life and from many countries flocked to his community when it began in 1825. Intellectually and socially, the community succeeded, but economically, it floundered from the start, failing completely in 1827. Owen, suffering from the hostility of much of the American public because of his aggressive assaults upon religion, eventually returned to England. A number of books have been written about the New Harmony experiment; see references 198, 213, 220, 228, 235, 240, and 246.

* * *

More than twenty freethought magazines appeared during this period, including some that lasted only a year or two, and others that ran for a decade or more. The most important magazines were *The Free*

Enquirer (186), *The Boston Investigator* (177), *The Correspondent* (184), and *The Beacon* (175).

The earliest freethought paper of the period was *The Free Enquirer,* which began in the New Harmony, Indiana, colony and was published first as the *New Harmony Gazette* (186) from October 1, 1825, to October 22, 1828. From 1828 until February 25, 1829, it was called *The New Harmony Gazette or Free Enquirer.* The magazine was then moved to New York City, where it was published as *The Free Enquirer* until 1835. Some of the people who served as editors of the magazine were Robert Dale Owen, Frances Wright, Robert L. Jennings, and H. D. Robinson. *The Free Enquirer* vigorously discussed such problems as religion, politics, sociology, and education. The magazine is discussed in *A History of Magazines, 1741-1850,* Vol. 1 (214) by Frank Luther Mott.

The next freethought journal was *The Correspondent* (184), which was begun in New York City by George Houston in 1827. This weekly publication lasted from January 20, 1827, to July 18, 1829. According to the prospectus, "the object contemplated by this journal is the diffusion of correct principles, which alone form the basis of morals and happiness. . . . There is still wanting a paper which will fearlessly advocate the paramount importance of the laws of nature and the dignity of reason."

Perhaps the most successful freethought magazine of the period was *The Boston Investigator* (177), which was begun by Abner Kneeland in 1831. It was "devoted to the development and promotion of universal mental liberty." The publishers were Abner Kneeland (1831-1838), Josiah Mendum (1839-1891), and Ernest Mendum (1892-1904). During its long life, it had only three editors: Abner Kneeland (1831-1839), Horace Seaver (1839-1889), and Lemuel K. Washburn (1889-1904).

The Beacon (175) was begun under the supervision of the Board of Directors of the United States Moral and Philosophical Society in New York on October 22, 1836. Gilbert Vale was the first editor, and after six months, he took the paper over completely. Vale published *The Beacon* on a weekly basis for several years, with the last issue appearing on December 19, 1846.

An excellent little freethought magazine that was published in New York City from 1848 to 1851, with Peter Eckler as the editor, was the *Age of Reason* (172). Eckler was one of the most important publishers of freethought literature during the second half of the nineteenth century. (For more on Eckler, see Chapter 3.)

The Western Examiner (237) was a "journal embodying a full and impartial enquiry into the truth or falsity of the Christian religion whether philosophically or historically viewed." It was published in St. Louis by John Bobb and lasted from January 1834 to December 10, 1835.

Other freethought magazines of this era included *The Comet* (181), *The Delaware Free Press* (185), *The Herald of Reason and Common Sense* (192), *The Liberal Advocate* (204), *The Liberal Press or Anti-Superstitionist* (205), *The Louisville Skeptic* (206), *The March of Mind* (209), *The Mohawk Liberal* (212), *The Regenerator* (221), *The Self Examiner* (224), *The Temple of Reason* (234), and *The World As It Is* (242). For further information on these publications, see the bibliography at the end of this chapter.

In 1856, John Shertzer Hittell (1825-1901), the California historian, wrote an extremely strong anti-Christian book entitled *The Evidences Against Christianity* (194). Hittell analyzed the books of the Bible, denied the existence of the Deity, and stated that "the Church must go." A biographical sketch of Hittell can be found in the *Dictionary of American Biography* (79).

*　*　*

The year 1825 marked a resurgence in both the freethought movement and in the freethought press. When Frances Wright and Robert Dale Owen published *The Free Enquirer* (186), they made an innovation in U.S. freethought publishing because they printed extracts from the freethought classics in their magazine. Later, they reprinted as books the series of freethought extracts that had been run in many issues. In this manner, they formed the first real U.S. freethought publishing company. The books they published bear the imprint "Wright and Owen," sometimes followed by "At the Office of the Free Enquirer." Among the books on their list were Paine's *The Age of Reason* (125), Baron D'Holbach's *Good Sense* (99), Frances Wright's and Robert Owen's works, and Shelley's *Queen Mab* (225).

One of Owen's assistants at *The Free Enquirer* was Augustus J. Matsell, who later opened a "liberal bookstore" and, along with G. W. Matsell (a relative, but the exact relationship is unknown), soon began printing his own editions of freethought books. The Matsells began publishing in about 1835. They published D'Holbach's *The System of Nature* (100), *Ecce Homo* (195), and *Good Sense* (99) as well as editions of Shelley's *Queen Mab* (225), Frances Wright's *A Few Days in Athens* (245) and her *Lectures* (244), Volney's *Ruins* (160), Robert Dale Owen's *Moral Physiology* (216), Robert Taylor's *Diegesis* (233), Voltaire's *Philosophical Dictionary* (161), Paine's *The Age of Reason* (125), and Kneeland's *A Review of the Evidences of Christianity*

(199). If the work was issued from "stereotype plates," the same plates were often used to reprint the book for many years and through a succession of liberal publishers.

H. D. Robinson (a pseudonym for H. M. Duhecquet) was an Englishman who settled in the United States and entered the publishing business in New York in about 1832. He translated some of D'Holbach's works from the original French into English. Many of his freethought publications were issued as a part of the "New York Philosophical Library" series.

It should be mentioned at this point that whenever one of these freethought publishers issued a popular book in an American edition, most of their contemporary freethought publishers would also sell the book (with the original publisher's imprint most of the time, but occasionally, by some agreement, with their own imprint). Two publishers who seemed to specialize in sharing the Matsells' publications with them were W. Sinclair of Philadelphia and G. H. Evans of Granville, New Jersey. Each of these, however, also published books on his own.

In 1831, Abner Kneeland began to publish *The Boston Investigator* (177), and he soon added a series of freethought books. The earliest of these bear the imprint "Published by Abner Kneeland at the Office of *The Boston Investigator*." Still later, after about 1840, the company became known as J. P. Mendum (see Chapter 3). Kneeland also published his own *Review of the Evidences of Christianity* (199) and *National Hymns* (200), as well as the first complete edition of Voltaire's *Philosophical Dictionary* (161) in English, for which Kneeland wrote the notes. He also published an edition of Paine's *The Age of Reason* (125) and sold the books of other freethought publishers.

Gilbert Vale, who nearly always referred to himself as G. Vale, set himself up as a freethought editor and publisher in about 1836 in New York City. He published editions of Strauss's *Life of Jesus* (230), Knowlton's *Elements of Modern Materialism* (201), Volney's *Ruins* (160), Shelley's *Queen Mab* (225), and Lyell's *Lectures on Geology* (207), among other books. He also had a series of freethought pamphlets, and, of course, editions of Paine's works. Many of these were the ones published by G. H. Evans at about this time.

* * *

As mentioned in Chapter 1, the Unitarian church grew out of the liberalizing tendencies within the Congregational church. The name "Unitarian" was only slowly and reluctantly accepted. The growth of Unitarianism was hastened by the appointment of Henry Ware, a liberal, as professor of theology at Harvard University in 1805. The Unitarian church continued to grow under the able leadership of William Ellery Channing (1780-1842). The spiritual call to arms of the Unitarian movement was given by Channing at the installation of Reverend Jared Sparks at the church in Baltimore in 1819. In 1825, the American Unitarian Association was formed. During this period, the church was loosely organized and its fundamental principles were not clearly settled. It was not until 1865 that a national conference was organized. The Unitarians have never adopted a creed and do not require either their members or ministers to profess a particular doctrine. The constitution of the General Conference simply stated that "These churches accept the religion of Jesus, holding in accordance with His teachings that practical religion is summed up in love of God and love of man."

The Universalist church developed in the United States under the leadership of John Murray, Elhanan Winchester, and others. During the first half of the nineteenth century, Hosea Ballou (1781-1852) became the recognized leader of the movement, and its most honored and influential exponent. During his ministry, the number of Universalist churches increased from some 20 or 30 to 500, distributed over New England, New York, Pennsylvania, Indiana, and Illinois.

The second quarter of the nineteenth century witnessed the development of Transcendentalism. On September 19, 1836, George Ripley of Boston called together a small group which included Amos Bronson Alcott, Ralph Waldo Emerson, and Frederick Henry Hedge "to see how far it would be possible for earnest minds to meet." All of those attending had a Unitarian background. They felt that the time had come to formulate a new and more vital faith than any that America then had. They believed Transcendentalism was the answer to a narrow and prematurely orthodox Unitarianism. The movement was confined principally to New England and flourished for a few years. In addition to those already listed, others more or less associated with the movement included Theodore Parker, Margaret Fuller, Orestes Bronson, Henry David Thoreau, Nathaniel Hawthorne, Charles Anderson Dana, and Elizabeth Palmer Peabody. They established Brook Farm, which existed for a few years during the 1840's. For the story of Brook Farm, see Lindsay Swift, *Brook Farm, Its Members, Scholars, and Visitors* (232) and Edith Roelker, *A Season in Utopia, The Story of Brook Farm* (223).

Additional information on Unitarianism, Universalism, and Transcendentalism may be found in references 9, 67, 165, 176, 178, 183, 188, 189, 196, 218, 222, 238, and 243.

Gerrit Smith (1797-1874) also made a contribution to the freethought movement. Following his graduation from Hamilton College in New York State, he became a lawyer, practicing his profession with distinction. He was elected to Congress in 1853. Inheriting a large fortune from his father, he used it for many philanthropic causes. After he became disillusioned with the Presbyterian church, he set up his own church in Peterboro, New York. In a series of discourses Smith delivered in his church in Peterboro between 1858 and 1861, he revealed a number of unorthodox positions; namely, he did not believe in miracles, hell, and many other religious concepts he considered contrary to reason. Smith claimed that church creeds were nothing but superstition. His church flourished for a while but finally dwindled away. In later life, he became a Methodist.

Smith's discourses were printed in *Religion of Reason* (226), and a collection of his speeches was published in *Sermons and Speeches of Gerrit Smith* (227). Biographies are *Gerrit Smith: Philanthropist and Reformer* (191) by Ralph Volney Harlow, and *Gerrit Smith: A Biography* (187) by Octavius Brooks Frothingham; a short biography appears in *Dictionary of American Biography* (79).

BIBLIOGRAPHY

172. *Age of Reason,* a biweekly freethought periodical published in New York City by Peter Eckler, 1848-1851.

173. Angle, Paul M. *Herndon's Life of Lincoln.* Greenwich, Conn.: Fawcett Publications, 1961.

174. *Appleton's Cyclopedia of American Biography.* New York: D. Appleton & Co., 1889.

175. *Beacon, The,* a weekly freethought journal published in New York City by Gilbert Vale, 1836-1846.

176. Blake, Nelson Manfred. *A History of American Life and Thought.* New York: McGraw-Hill Co., 1963.

177. *Boston Investigator, The,* a weekly freethought newspaper published in Boston, 1831-1904. For further information, see narration above.

178. Brauer, Gerald C. *Protestantism in America, A Narrative History.* Philadelphia: Westminster Press, 1953.

179. Brigance, William Norwood, ed. *A History and Criticism of American Public Address,* Vol. 1. New York: McGraw-Hill Book Co., 1943. Contains an evaluation of Frances Wright, Ernestine L. Rose, and Robert G. Ingersoll as public lecturers.

180. Cardiff, Ira D. *The Truth About Lincoln.* Boston: Christopher Publishing House, 1943.

181. *Comet, The,* a weekly freethought periodical published every Thursday in New York City by H. D. Robinson (pseudonym of H. M. Duhecquet), 1832-1833.

182. Commager, Henry Steele. "The Blasphemy of Abner Knee-land." *New England Quarterly* 8 (1935):29-41. Kneeland also published reports of his own trials in a series of pamphlets.

183. Commager, Henry Steele. *Theodore Parker.* Boston: Beacon Press, 1947.

184. *Correspondent, The,* a weekly freethought periodical published in New York City by George Houston, 1827-1829.

185. *Delaware Free Press, The,* a freethought periodical published in Wilmington, Delaware, by Benjamin Webb and Dr. W. W. Baker, 1830-1833.

186. *Free Enquirer, The,* a weekly freethought periodical first published as *The New Harmony Gazette* in New Harmony, Indiana, 1825-1828. After this time, its name was changed to *The New Harmony Gazette or Free Enquirer.* The magazine moved to New York in 1829, with the title *The Free Enquirer.* It ceased publication in 1835.

187. Frothingham, Octavius B. *Gerrit Smith: A Biography.* New York: G. P. Putnam's Sons, 1878.

188. Frothingham, Octavius B. *Transcendentalism in New England.* New York: G. P. Putnam's Sons, 1876.

189. Gohdes, Clarence. *Periodicals of American Transcendentalism.* Durham, N.C.: University of North Carolina Press, 1931.

190. Graham, Andrew J., ed. *Proceedings of the Hartford Bible Convention.* New York: Published by the Committee, 1854.

191. Harlow, Ralph Volney, *Gerrit Smith: Philanthropist and Reformer.* New York: Henry Holt & Co., 1939.

192. *Herald of Reason and Common Sense, The,* a freethought periodical published at Poughkeepsie, New York, by Jesse Torrey, Jr., 1835.

193. Hertell, Thomas. *The Spirit of Truth: Being an Exposition of Infidelity or Religious Belief.* Boston: J. P. Mendum, 1845.

194. Hittell, John Shertzer. *The Evidences Against Christianity.* San Francisco: Published by the Author, 1856, 2 vols.

195. Holbach, Paul Henry Thiry, Baron D'. *Ecce Homo.* New York: Printed for the Proprietors of the Philosophical Society, 1827. This was the first American edition. The first English translation was issued as London: "Printed For the Booksellers," 1799. The first edition of this work was published in 1770, in French, under the title *Histoire Critique de Jésus-Christ,* [Amsterdam: M. M. Rey].

196. Hutchinson, William R. *The Transcendentalist Ministers.* New Haven: Yale University Press, 1959.

197. Ingram, H. A. *Life and Character of Stephen Girard.* Philadelphia: E. S. Hart, 1885.

198. Johnson, Oakley C. *Robert Owen in the United States.* New York: Humanities Press, 1970. Contains an introductory essay by Johnson and three important speeches given by Owen in the United States. Has an excellent bibliography.

199. Kneeland, Abner. *A Review of the Evidences of Christianity.* New York: no publisher, 1829.

200. Kneeland, Abner, ed. *National Hymns, Original and Selected, for the Use of Those Who Are "Slaves to No Sect."* Boston: Office of the Investigator, 1836.

201. Knowlton, Charles. *Elements of Modern Materialism.* Adams, Mass.: Published by the Author, 1829.

202. Lane, Margaret. *Frances Wright and the "Great Experiment."* Totowa, N.J.: Rowman & Littlefield, 1972.

203. Leopold, Richard William. *Robert Dale Owen, A Biography.* Cambridge, Mass.: Harvard University Press, 1940.

204. *Liberal Advocate, The,* a freethought periodical published at Rochester, N.Y., by Obediah Dogberry, 1832-1834.

205. *Liberal Press or Anti-Superstitionist, The,* a freethought periodical published by The Society of Liberal Friends, Philadelphia, 1828.

206. *Louisville Skeptic, The,* a freethought periodical published in Louisville, Ky., by R.K.M. Ormsby, 1838.

207. Lyell, Sir Charles. *Lectures on Geology.* New York: Greely & McElrath, 1843.

208. Malone, Dumas. *The Public Life of Thomas Cooper, 1783-1839.* New Haven: Yale University Press, 1926.

209. *March of Mind, The,* a freethought journal published in Cincinnati, 1828.

210. *Meteor of Light, Containing the Minutes of the Proceedings of the Infidel Convention Held in the City of New York, May 4th, 5th and 6th, 1845.* Boston: J. P. Mendum, 1845.

211. *Minutes of the Infidel Convention Held in the City of Philadelphia, Sept. 7th and 8th, 1857.* Philadelphia: Published by the Central Committee, 1858.

212. *Mohawk Liberal, The,* a freethought periodical published at Little Falls, N.Y., by L. Windsor Smith, 1833-1834.

213. Morton, A. L. *The Life and Ideas of Robert Owen.* New York: Monthly Review Press, 1963.

214. Mott, Frank Luther. *A History of Magazines, 1741-1850,* Vol. 1. Cambridge, Mass.: Harvard University Press, 1939.

215. Offen, Benjamin. *A Legacy to the Friends of Free Discus-*

sion: Being a Review of the Principal Historical Facts and Personages of the Books Known as the Old and New Testament, With Remarks on the Morality of Nature. Boston: J. P. Mendum, 1846.

216. Owen, Robert Dale. Moral Physiology. New York: Wright & Owen, 1831.

217. Owen, Robert Dale. Twenty-seven Years of Autobiography, Threading My Way. New York: G. W. Carleton & Co., 1874. The British edition (London: Trüber, "1874") was really published in 1873.

218. Parke, David B. The Epic of Unitarianism: Original Writings from the History of Liberal Religion. Boston: Starr King Press, 1957.

219. Perkins, A.J.G., and Wolfson, Theresa. Frances Wright: Free Enquirer. New York: Harper & Bros., 1939.

220. Pitzer, Donald E., ed. Robert Owen's Legacy. Proceedings of the Robert Owen Bicentennial Conference. Indianapolis: Indiana Historical Society, 1972.

221. Regenerator, The, a freethought periodical published at Fruit Hills, Ohio, by Orson S. Murray, 1844-1848.

222. Rice, Madeleine Hook. Federal Street Pastor, The Life of William Ellery Channing. New York: Bookman Associates, 1961.

223. Roelker, Edith. A Season in Utopia, The Story of Brook Farm. New York: Thomas Nelson & Sons, 1961.

224. Self Examiner, The, a freethought periodical published at Goshen, Ohio, by Aaron Hinchman, 1843.

225. Shelley, Percy Bysshe. Queen Mab. New York: Wright & Owen, 1831.

226. Smith, Gerrit. Religion of Reason. New York: American News Co., 1864. An earlier version was called Three Discourses on the Religion of Reason.

227. Smith, Gerrit. Sermons and Speeches of Gerrit Smith. New York: Ross & Tousey, 1861.

228. Snedeker, Caroline Dale. The Town of the Fearless. Garden City, N.Y.: Doubleday, Doran & Co., 1931.

229. Stiller, Richard. Commune on the Frontier, The Story of Frances Wright. New York: Thomas Y. Crowell, 1972.

230. Strauss, David Friedrich. The Life of Jesus Critically Examinded. Tübingen, Germany: C. F. Osiander, 1835-1836, 2 vols. First American edition was New York: C. Blanchard, 1855.

231. Suhl, Yuri. Ernestine L. Rose and the Battle for Human Rights. New York: Reynal & Co., 1959. Rose wrote little herself. Perhaps her most pertinent statement of her beliefs on religion can be found in her pamphlet A Defense of Atheism (Boston: J. P. Mendum, 1889).

232. Swift, Lindsay. *Brook Farm, Its Members, Scholars, and Visitors.* New York: Macmillan Co., 1900.

233. Taylor, Robert. *Diegesis.* London: R. Carlile, 1829. First American edition was Boston: J. Gilbert, 1832.

234. *Temple of Reason, The,* a freethought periodical published in Philadelphia by Russell Canfield, 1835-1837.

235. Tyler, Alice Felt. *Freedom's Ferment,* Minneapolis: University of Minnesota Press, 1944.

236. Waterman, William R. *Frances Wright.* New York: Columbia University Press, 1924.

237. *Western Examiner, The,* a freethought periodical published in St. Louis by John Bobb, 1835.

238. Whicher, George F., ed. *The Transcendentalist Revolt Against Materialism.* Boston: D. C. Heath & Co., 1949.

239. Wildes, Harry Emerson. *Lonely Midas, The Story of Stephen Girard.* New York: Farrar & Rinehart, 1943.

240. Wilson, William E. *The Angel and the Serpent, The Story of New Harmony.* Bloomington, Ind.: Indiana University Press, 1946.

241. Wolf, William J. *The Almost Chosen People.* New York: Doubleday & Co., 1959. Reprinted as *The Religion of Abraham Lincoln.* New York: Seabury Press, 1963.

242. *World As It Is, The,* a freethought periodical published at Rochester, N.Y., by Dr. Luke Shepherd, 1836.

243. Wright, Conrad. *Three Prophets of Religious Liberalism, Channing, Emerson, Parker.* Boston: Beacon Press, 1961.

244. Wright, Frances. *A Course of Popular Lectures.* New York: Free Enquirer, 1829. Expanded versions published in 1831 and 1836.

245. Wright, Frances. *A Few Days in Athens.* London: Hurst, Rees, Orme & Brown, 1822. First American edition was New York: Wright & Owen, 1831.

246. Young, Marguerite. *Angel in the Forest, A Fairy Tale of Two Utopias.* New York: Reynal & Hitchcock, 1945.

3.

★★★★★★★★★

The Golden Age
of Freethought

The golden age of freethought, which began about the time of the Civil War and ended shortly after the death of Robert G. Ingersoll (i.e., 1860-1900), is the period of the greatest freethought activity in the history of the United States. During this period, more freethought organizations, local and national, existed, more magazines and books were published, and, most importantly, the greatest active freethinker America produced, Robert G. Ingersoll, lived and worked for freethought.

The indispensable book on this period is Sidney Warren's *American Freethought, 1860-1914* (44), a comprehensive volume that carefully explores the leading personalities, organizations, magazines, and principal activities of the time, and also provides an excellent bibliography. Thorough coverage of the period is also provided in George E. Macdonald's *Fifty Years of Freethought* (23), the story of *The Truth Seeker* (343) during 1875-1900 (as well as into the twentieth century), and Samuel Porter Putnam's *Four Hundred Years of Freethought* (30). Putnam's book is probably the best one on the freethought organizations and personalities of the second half of the nineteenth century.

The principal personalities in the freethought movement during its golden age were Benjamin Franklin Underwood, Robert Green Ingersoll, DeRobigne M. Bennett, Samuel Porter Putnam, Henry L. Green, Charles B. Reynolds, John E. Remsburg, Thaddeus Burr Wakeman, and Eugene M. Macdonald. Many more did yeoman service in the cause of freethought, but these are the most important.

Benjamin Franklin Underwood (1839-1914) was born in New York City. He supplemented the meager education he received in the common schools and the Westerly Academy (Rhode Island) by wide reading in philosophy, science, and literature. After serving in the

Civil War, he became an effective freethought lecturer. In the 1870s and 1880s, he terrorized the churches of the East by his custom of challenging the clergy of the large cities to meet him in a debate. The series of debates ran from three to as many as thirty sessions.

Underwood traveled throughout the United States for a number of years giving freethought lectures, many of which were reprinted as pamphlets. Some of the more than thirty lectures include "The Theory of Evolution," "The Genesis and Nature of Religion," "Modern Scientific Materialism," "The Pros and Cons of a Future State," "Crimes and Cruelties of Christianity," "Paine the Pioneer of Freethought in America," "Science Versus the Bible," and "The Four Gospels Unhistorical and Unreliable."

From 1881 to 1886, Underwood edited *The Index* (309) in Boston, and in 1887 he edited *The Open Court* (328). From 1887 to 1913, the year in which he retired, Underwood was the editor of a newspaper in Quincy, Illinois. The only biography of Underwood is in the *Dictionary of American Biography* (79).

Robert Green Ingersoll (1833-1899), born at Dresden, New York, was by far the greatest freethinker of the period. His father was a minister who was frequently moved from church to church; during Robert's boyhood, his father served churches in New York, Ohio, Wisconsin, and Illinois. While in Illinois, Ingersoll studied law and was admitted to the bar. He became a highly successful attorney in practice with his brother Ebon in Peoria. In 1862, he married Eva Parker, also a freethinker. During the Civil War, Ingersoll was commissioned colonel of the Eleventh Illinois Cavalry; he was captured and later paroled.

As a skillful public speaker, Ingersoll was frequently asked to give public lectures. The first lecture in which he revealed his agnosticism was entitled "Progress," delivered in 1860. Other freethought lectures which he prepared and delivered to huge audiences all over the United States included "Thomas Paine" (1870), "The Gods" (1872), "Heretics and Heresies" (1874), "The Liberty of Man, Woman and Child" (1877), "Ghosts" (1877), "Some Mistakes of Moses" (1879), "What Must We Do to Be Saved" (1880), "The Great Infidels" (1881), "Orthodoxy" (1884), "Myth and Miracle" (1885), "Voltaire" (1894), "The Holy Bible" (1894), "Why I am an Agnostic" (1896), and "What Is Religion?" (1899). The dates given are only those years in which the speeches were first delivered or first published; some of the speeches were given many years before and after publication.

Ingersoll, one of the most brilliant orators of all time, could hold the attention of thousands of people for hours. For an evaluation of

Ingersoll as an orator, see *A History and Criticism of American Public Address* (179).

Ingersoll moved from Peoria to Washington, D.C., in 1877 and in 1885, he moved to New York City, where he spent the remainder of his life. He died at his son-in-law's home in Dobbs Ferry, New York, on July 21, 1899. Mrs. Ingersoll died in 1923. Their remains were buried in Arlington National Cemetery (Section 3, Grave 1620), where the impressive grave marker contains the Ingersoll quotation: "Nothing is grander than to break chains from the bodies of men/Nothing nobler than to destroy phantoms of the soul." A statue of Ingersoll was erected in Peoria in 1911.

Ingersoll's beliefs are best summarized by a quotation from his collected works (311), published in twelve volumes (vol. 8, pp. 246-247):

Question: Do you believe in the existence of a Supreme Being?
Answer: I do not believe in any Supreme personality or in any Supreme Being who made the universe and governs nature. I do not say that there is no such Being—all I say is that I do not believe that such a Being exists. I know nothing on the subject, except that I know that I do not know and that nobody else knows. But if there be such a Being, he certainly never wrote the Old Testament. You will understand my position. I do not say that a Supreme Being does not exist, but I do say that I do not believe such a Being exists. The universe—embracing all that is—all atoms, all stars, each grain of sand and all the constellations, each thought and dream of animals and man, all matter and all force, all doubt and all belief, all virtue and all crime, all joy and all pain, all growth and all decay—is all there is. It does not act because it is moved from without. It acts from within. It is actor and subject, means and end.
It is infinite; the infinite could not be created. It is indestructible and that which cannot be destroyed was not created. I am a Pantheist.

Question: Don't you think the belief of the Agnostic is more satisfactory to the believer than that of the Atheist?
Answer: There is no difference. The Agnostic is an Atheist. The Atheist is an Agnostic. The Agnostic says: "I do not know, but I do not believe there is a God." The Atheist says the same. The orthodox Christian says he knows there is a God; but we know that he does not know. He simply believes. He cannot know. The Atheist cannot know that God does not exist.

Ingersoll's humanitarian creed can best be summarized as follows: (1) Happiness is the only good, (2) the place to be happy is here, (3) the time to be happy is now, and (4) the way to be happy is to make others so.

Many books have been written about Ingersoll, the most important of which is Gordon Stein's *Robert G. Ingersoll: A Checklist* (39). This volume lists the various editions of Ingersoll's own writings, books he contributed to, his articles, articles and books about him, including biographies, as well as translations of his works. There are nearly 1,000 entries.

The Works of Robert G. Ingersoll (311), often called the Dresden Edition, was published in 1900 in twelve volumes arranged as follows: volumes 1-4, Lectures; 5-7, Discussions; 8, Interviews; 9, Political; 10, Legal; 11-12, Miscellany. In 1911, a thirteenth volume was added: *Ingersoll: A Biographical Appreciation* (314) by Herman Kittredge.

Joseph Lewis, about whom more will be said later, collected many of Ingersoll's most important sayings in a 569-page volume entitled *Ingersoll the Magnificent* (317). *The Letters of Robert G. Ingersoll* (345), edited by Eva Ingersoll Wakefield, contains many of the letters Ingersoll wrote to members of his family, plus a biographical sketch.

There have been a number of full-length biographies of Ingersoll. Among the best are *Royal Bob* (278) by C. H. Cramer and *American Infidel: Robert G. Ingersoll* (315) by Orvin Larson. Other biographies are cited in references 254, 280, 301, 314, 320, and 338.

DeRobigne Mortimer Bennett (1818-1882) tried his hand at many different vocations. While in the seed business at Paris, Illinois, he decided to publish a freethought newspaper, which he named *The Truth Seeker* (343), because he felt that the local press had not given him fair treatment in a controversy he had had with two clergy-men over the utility of prayer. The Paris paper had printed the clergy-men's responses, but refused to publish Bennett's view that prayer was futile. Bennett's paper was successful, and shortly thereafter he moved it to New York City. *The Truth Seeker* has been published continuously since it first appeared in 1873. In addition to editing and publishing his paper, Bennett was a prolific writer. Among his works are *The World's Sages, Infidels and Thinkers* (6), *The Champions of the Church* (257), and *A Truth Seeker Around the World* (260). Bennett was active in freethought circles from 1873 to 1882 and was extraordinarily productive in these years. Bennett spent a year in jail, after mailing two sex/birth control pamphlets to Anthony Comstock (who had tricked him into doing so by using a decoy name and address), and he even used that year to write a large two-volume work. Biograph-ical sketches of Bennett are given in *Four Hundred Years of Free-thought* (30), the *Dictionary of American Biography* (79), and *A Biographical Dictionary of Modern Rationalists* (24). No full biography has ever been written.

Another active freethinker of this period was an ex-minister named Samuel Porter Putnam (1838-1896). After his service in the Civil

War, Putnam became first a Congregational and then a Unitarian minister. After a few years as a Unitarian minister, he gave up all connection whatsoever with the Christian religion and became a freethinker, devoting the remainder of his life to the cause of freethought. He was elected secretary of the American Secular Union and later became president of that organization. In 1888, he, along with George E. Macdonald, established the magazine *Freethought* (291) in San Francisco. That magazine lasted until 1891.

Putnam traveled over 100,000 miles into all but four states lecturing on freethought. He was the founder and president of the Freethought Federation of America. In addition to writing several pamphlets and poetry, he wrote *Four Hundred Years of Freethought* (30). Putnam's wide travel and knowledge of the people and organizations active in the freethought movement make his book the best available on these subjects. Biographical sketches appear in references 24 and 30.

Henry L. Green (1828-1903), a self-educated man, spent some time as a farmer, log rafter, school teacher, lawyer, politician, justice of the peace, and anti-slavery speaker. He became associated with the freethought movement in the late 1870s and was chosen corresponding secretary of the New York Freethinkers' Association, planning and managing their convention for a number of years. He established and edited *The Freethinkers' Magazine* (290), which was published in Buffalo, New York, from 1882 to 1894. After 1894, it moved to Chicago, with the name changed to *Freethought Magazine* (292), and was published there until 1903.

Charles B. Reynolds (1832-1896), originally a Seventh Day Adventist minister, left that church to become a freethought lecturer. He made his first appearance in that capacity at the New York Freethinkers' Convention of 1883, where he gave an excellent eulogy to the late D. M. Bennett. Reynolds held his freethought lectures in tents. At one of those tent meetings in Boonton, New Jersey, in 1886, he was arrested for blasphemy. Despite an eloquent defense by Robert G. Ingersoll, he was found guilty and fined. Late in life, Reynolds went West, where he lectured in Washington and Oregon. Biographical sketches of Reynolds appear in references 24 and 30.

John Eleazer Remsburg (1848-1919) was one of the most active lecturers and most prolific freethought writers of this era. Following his service in the Civil War, he taught school and then served as superintendent of public instruction for Atchinson County, Kansas. In 1880, he published *Thomas Paine: The Apostle of Religious and Political Liberty* (137). The year 1880 also marks the beginning of Remsburg's career as a freethought lecturer. By the time of his retirement twenty years later, he had traveled 360,000 miles to deliver more than 3,000 lectures in 52 states, territories, or provinces, as well as 1,250 cities and towns of the United States and Canada. Remsburg wrote three other important freethought books: *The Bible* (333), *The Christ* (334), and *Six Historic Americans* (32). Biographical sketches of Remsburg are in references 24 and 30.

One of the most scholarly freethinkers of the period was Thaddeus Burr Wakeman (1834-1913). He attended Princeton University (where he graduated with honors in 1854) in order to enter the ministry; instead he became a rationalist. He turned to law and practiced in New York City with great success. He served as President of the National Liberal League for three years and as president of the New York Freethinkers in 1897. In addition to editing the freethought magazine *Man* (321), Wakeman was president of the Liberal University in Silverton, Oregon. He was a perennial convention speaker and delivered the funeral addresses for many of the prominent freethinkers of the era. For biographical sketches of Wakeman, see references 23, 24, and 30.

Eugene Montague Macdonald (1855-1909) succeeded D. M. Bennett as editor of *The Truth Seeker* (343) and held that position for twenty-six years. During his editorship, *The Truth Seeker* became the leading freethought journal in America. Macdonald was very active in the American Secular Union and became president of that organization. He wrote *Col. Robert G. Ingersoll As He Is* (320).

Other important freethought lecturers, writers, or organizational workers of the 1860-1899 period included William S. Bell, Helen Hamilton Gardener, Kersey Graves, John Peck, Horace Seaver, Edwin C. Walker, Elizur Wright, Lemuel K. Washburn, and James L. York. Information on these freethinkers may be obtained in references 23 and 30.

Although not directly connected with the freethought movement, Samuel L. Clemens (1835-1910), better known as Mark Twain, was a freethinker. Very early in life, he began to doubt the truth of his religious teachings and finally rejected orthodox religion. He believed in God but did not believe in the Bible as the word of God, and he questioned man's immortality. Twain gave expression to his skepticism in the following works: *Christian Science* (271), *Letters from the Earth* (272), *The Mysterious Stranger* (273), *Report from Paradise* (274), and *What Is Man?* (275). A number of books and articles have been written about Twain's religion; see references 283, 288, 300, 303, 326, and 339.

John Fiske (1842-1901), historian, lecturer, and philosopher, did much to popularize the theory of evolution during the late nineteenth century. He accepted an "unknowable" God, believed in immortality as an act of faith, and rejected Christian doctrines. Through his *Outlines of Cosmic Philosophy* (286), Fiske attempted to reconcile evolutionary development with his theistic beliefs. For biographies of Fiske and books describing his religious beliefs, consult references 262, 329, 348, and 349.

* * *

In 1876, freethinkers again attempted to form a national organization; this organization, the National Liberal League, met first in Philadelphia and lasted longer than any other national freethought organization. (The name was changed to the American Secular Union in 1883.) It held annual congresses in the following cities: Philadelphia (1876, 1889, 1891), Rochester (1877), Syracuse (1878), Cincinnati (1879), Chicago (1880, 1881, 1887, 1892, 1893, 1894, 1896, 1898, 1910), St. Louis (1882, 1904), Milwaukee (1883), Cassadaga, New York (1884), Cleveland (1885), Pittsburgh (1888), Portsmouth, Ohio (1890), Boston (1899), Buffalo (1901), and Brooklyn (1902). Presidents of the organization included Francis E. Abbot, Elizur Wright, Thaddeus B. Wakeman, Robert G. Ingersoll, Courtland Palmer, Samuel P. Putnam, Richard B. Westbrook, Charles B. Waite, John E. Remsburg, Eugene M. Macdonald, E. P. Peacock and Marshall Gauvin.

At these annual conventions, such topics as secularist legislation, Bible reading in the public schools, taxation of church property, and Sunday closing laws were the chief concerns. In order to promote the goals of the American Secular Union, local subsidiary organizations were encouraged. At one time, more than 200 of these were listed, although only a few were effective.

In 1894, the American Secular Union merged with the Freethought Federation of America, a national organization formed in 1892 mainly through the efforts of Samuel P. Putnam. After the turn of the century, the American Secular Union was definitely in its decline: it held few congresses and, finally, just a board of directors met to choose the officers of the organization. In the 1920s, it ceased to exist altogether.

A successful local organization was the New York Freethinkers' Association, founded in 1877. For a number of years it held annual conventions attended by large audiences and addressed by the leading freethinkers of the country.

For additional information on freethought organizations, both local and national, see references 23, 30, and 44. See also the Golden Jubilee Number of *The Truth Seeker* (September 1, 1923), a special

sixty-four page edition which traces the history of freethought from
1873 to 1923.

* * *

In 1881, George H. Walser (1834-1910) founded a town for
freethinkers named Liberal in Barton County, Missouri, in which there
were to be no priests, preachers, churches, saloons, God, or hell.
Walser started a freethought university in the town and published a
newspaper named *The Liberal* (318). Before his death in 1910,
Walser turned to Spiritualism.

The story of Liberal is told in James Proctor Moore's *This Strange
Town—Liberal, Missouri* (325). See also *The Truth Seeker* for October
28, 1922, p. 687, and *Missouri: A Guide to the "Show Me" State*
(350), p. 504.

The Boston Investigator (177) continued to be one of the leading
freethought periodicals during the 1860-1899 period. Horace Seaver
(1810-1889) was the editor from 1839 to 1889, when he was succeeded by Lemuel K. Washburn. *The Boston Investigator* reached a
maximum circulation of about 6,000.

The Index (309) was published by the Free Religious Association, first in Toledo, Ohio (1870-1872) and then in Boston (1873-
1886). In 1886, it merged with *The Open Court* (328). The successive
editors were Francis Ellingwood Abbot, W.J. Potter, and B.F. Underwood.

One of the most popular freethought magazines of the period
was *The Truth Seeker* (343), founded by D. M. Bennett and published in New York City during this time. Upon Bennett's death in
1882, Eugene Montague Macdonald became its editor and served
until his death. During Macdonald's editorship, the magazine reached
a circulation high of 9,000 (1894-1896). It was published weekly from
1876 to 1930 and monthly thereafter. The complete story of *The
Truth Seeker* is told in *Fifty Years of Freethought* (23) by George E.
Macdonald.

In 1882, Henry L. Green established *The Freethinkers' Magazine*
at Buffalo. It was published there through 1894, at which time it moved
to Chicago and changed its name to *Freethought Magazine* (292).
As such, it was published until 1903, when it merged with *The Torch
of Reason* (342). *Freethought Magazine* reached a circulation of
3,443 in 1897.

The Torch of Reason (342) was founded in 1896 in Silverton,
Oregon, by J. E. Hosmer and transferred to Kansas City, Missouri
in 1902. Thaddeus Burr Wakeman became editor in 1899. In 1904,
The Torch of Reason and *Freethought Magazine* merged to form

The Liberal Review (319) and in 1906, *The Liberal Review* was united with *The Open Road.*

The Blue Grass Blade (263) was a freethought weekly magazine published by Charles C. Moore in Lexington, Kentucky, from 1884 to 1885, after which it moved to Cincinnati until 1891. It was moved back to Lexington after that and continued to publish irregularly until the early 1900s. Moore was arrested, tried in 1899, found guilty, and sent to prison for publishing "obscene" material. He wrote about his case in his autobiography *Behind the Bars; 31498* (263).

The Independent Pulpit (308), a monthly freethought magazine, was founded in Waco, Texas, by J. D. Shaw and was issued from 1883 to 1910. Its name was changed to *The Searchlight* (335) in 1902. During 1889-1892, it reached a circulation high of over 2,000.

Man (321) was a freethought magazine edited by Thaddeus Burr Wakeman for the Board of Managers of the National Liberal League (New York City) from 1878 to 1884. (Wakeman's career is discussed above.)

Lester Frank Ward (1841-1913) published a monthly freethought magazine called *The Iconoclast* (307) from 1870 to 1871 in Washington, D.C. Ward later became one of America's most distinguished sociologists; his last years were spent as professor of sociology at Brown University. His definitive biography is *Lester F. Ward: The American Aristotle* (270) by Samuel Chugerman.

J. R. Monroe (1825-1891), an American physician who rendered devoted service during the Civil War, established *The Rockford Herald* in 1855 to support abolition and other reforms. He moved to Seymour, Indiana, in 1857 and founded *The Seymour Times.* In 1881, he moved his paper to Indianapolis and called it *The Ironclad Age* (312). This rationalist paper was an aggressive weekly and was popular with freethinkers. It had a circulation of over 3,000. Following Monroe's death in 1891, his daughter, Lulie Monroe Powers (1850-1895), continued its publication until her death. After that, it was published by P. H. and Pearl A. Powers until it was absorbed by *The Truth Seeker* (343) in 1898.

Other freethought magazines published during this era were for the most part local and usually lasted only briefly. Many of them are mentioned in *Four Hundred Years of Freethought* (30).

Two books that have been reprinted many times and have been favorites of freethinkers over the years were first published during this period: *The World's Sixteen Crucified Saviors* (302) by Kersey Graves (1813-1883) and *Bible Myths and Their Parallel in Other Religions* (281) by Thomas W. Doane (1851-1885).

The conflict between science and theology is the topic of two outstanding books: *History of the Conflict Between Religion and Science* (282) by John William Draper (1811-1882) and *A History of the Warfare of Science with Theology in Christendom* (347) by Andrew Dickson White (1832-1918). For a biography of Draper, see *John W. Draper* (287) by Donald Fleming; also see *Science and Religion in American Thought* (348) by Edward A. White. Andrew White was a distinguished historian and also the first president of Cornell University. For further information on White, see *The Autobiography of Andrew Dickson White* (346). *The Struggle Between Science and Superstition* (316) by Arthur M. Lewis and *Landmarks in the Struggle Between Science and Religion* (337) by James Young Simpson are both useful books for further information on the science-theology conflict.

Edgar Fawcett (1847-1904), poet and novelist, expressed his freethought point of view in his *Agnosticism and Other Essays* (284), with a Prologue by Robert G. Ingersoll. Stanley R. Harrison has written a biography of Fawcett entitled *Edgar Fawcett* (304).

Matilda Joslyn Gage (1826-1898), writer and woman suffragist, wrote *Woman, Church and State* (298), which was popular with freethinkers. Helen Hamilton Gardener (1853-1925), another woman freethinker, wrote the popular *Men, Women and Gods, and Other Lectures* (299), as well as several freethought novels.

Two popular novels dealing with the conflict between liberalism and strict orthodoxy in religion were *John Ward, Preacher* (279) by Margaret Deland and *The Damnation of Theron Ware* (289) by Harold Frederic. Both focus on the religious conflicts of preachers. For additional information on Margaret Deland and Harold Frederic, see references 266, 327, and 339.

* * *

We have mentioned that Abner Kneeland founded *The Boston Investigator* (177) in 1831 and that he also issued books from the magazine's offices. After Kneeland left for Iowa in 1838 to found a utopian colony, *The Boston Investigator* was taken over by Horace Seaver as editor and by Josiah P. Mendum as publisher. Mendum soon began publishing books as well, under the imprint J. P. Mendum. His company became one of the most important freethought publishers in nineteenth-century America. The company stayed in business until 1904, when it merged with the Truth Seeker Company.

Mendum published a wide variety of freethought books. Some were reprints of previously issued classics such as Paine's *The Age of Reason* (125), D'Holbach's *The System of Nature* (100) and *Good*

Sense (99), Volney's *Ruins* (160), Ethan Allen's *Reason the Only Oracle of Man* (51), and a few Voltaire items. Among the original books he published were the first American editions of Robert Taylor's *Syntagma* (341) and *The Devil's Pulpit* (340), D'Holbach's *Letters to Eugenia* (306), and Robert Cooper's *The Infidel's Text-Book* (277) and *Immortality of the Soul* (276). Mendum also published the first American edition of Bradlaugh et al.'s *Half-Hours with the Freethinkers* (265). Mendum cooperated with D. M. Bennett in the publication of W. H. Burr's *Revelations of Antichrist* (267), published anonymously. Mendum also published a large number of pamphlets. including some by John Remsburg, Ernestine Rose, and Thomas Hertell.

D. M. Bennett moved to New York City in 1873, bringing with him his year-old freethought journal, *The Truth Seeker.* In addition to publishing the journal, he was soon issuing books under his own imprint (D. M. Bennett). At first most of the books so issued were either classics such as Thomas Paine's works or American editions of British freethought books that had recently been published, such as Amberley's *Analysis of Religious Belief* (252) and W. R. Cassels' *Supernatural Religion* (269). Bennett himself was a prolific author, turning out several large biographical works (e.g., references 6 and 257), which he also published and sold. His articles in *The Truth Seeker,* along with the articles of others, were often reprinted as Bennett publications. Among these were his *Thirty Discussions* (259), bound volumes of *Truth Seeker Tracts* (261), and with G. H. Humphrey, *Christianity and Infidelity: The Humphrey-Bennett Discussions* (258).

After Bennett's sudden death in 1882, the Truth Seeker Company, as it was now called, continued to expand under the able direction of E. M. Macdonald, formerly a compositor working for Bennett. During 1883-1929, the Truth Seeker Company published literally hundreds of books and thousands of pamphlets. Hence only a brief list of the most significant new or original titles can be given here. (It should be noted that the Truth Seeker Company also reprinted the previously published works of other freethought publishers.)

Among the more significant titles were pamphlets by Ingersoll, W. S. Bell's *Handbook of Freethought* (256), Hirsch's *Religion and Civilization* (305), and the books listed in references 23, 30, 281, 333, and 334. The pamphlets must have included the work of every published American freethinker who wrote during the 1875-1920 period when the company was at its publishing peak.

During its period of rapid growth (1875-1880), the Truth Seeker Company absorbed several other small freethought publishing companies. One of these was C. P. Somerby's company. (Somerby subsequently became the business manager of the Truth Seeker Company.) Earlier, Somerby's company had republished a number of classics, such as W. Winwood Reade's *The Martyrdom of Man* (332), Bradlaugh's *A Few Words About the Devil* (264), the only American edition of a book entirely by Bradlaugh, and Feuerbach's *The Essence of Christianity* (285). Somerby also issued a number of original publications, among them Sara Underwood's *Heroines of Freethought* (344).

Another active publisher of the period was Peter Eckler. He began in 1842 as a printer for some of the other freethought publishers and remained the actual printer for many freethought books issued with other publishers' imprints on them (e.g., C. P. Farrell). Eckler also issued a large number of books and pamphlets under his own name, especially in the 1880-1915 period. Among the books he published were editions of nearly all the freethought classics (Paine, Volney, Voltaire, Higgins, etc.), many of which were issued with uniform brown bindings as part of the Library of Liberal Classics series. He also issued many of Ingersoll's lectures (see reference 39) and was the printer of most of the rest of the authorized editions. Eckler also sold the books of most other freethought publishers.

C. P. Farrell, Robert G. Ingersoll's brother-in-law, was Ingersoll's "authorized" publisher almost from the beginning. The first C. P. Farrell imprint appears on the 1874 edition of *The Gods and Other Lectures* (310), published in Peoria, Illinois. Farrell published almost all of Ingersoll's lectures, including the twelve-volume Dresden Edition of his collected works in 1900. A few of Ingersoll's pamphlets, mostly made up from articles he had written for *The Truth Seeker* magazine, were published by the Truth Seeker Company. Farrell published Ingersoll items almost exclusively; the one main exception was *A Short History of the Bible* (313) by Bronson Keeler. Farrell's last publication was probably I. Newton Baker's *An Intimate View of Robert G. Ingersoll* (255), published in 1920.

Among the relatively minor freethought publishers of the 1860-1899 period was the Freidenker Publishing Company of Milwaukee, which issued a number of freethought books and pamphlets in German for members of the Freie Gemeinde. Asa K. Butts of New York and later, New Jersey published a number of pamphlets and small books on sex worship and population limitation, including some by the British freethinker Annie Besant. J. W. Bouton of New York issued some American editions of scarce British freethought books, especially those of Thomas Inman. Like Butts, he seemed to specialize in books exploring the sexual elements in Christianity.

The publishers of two of the previously mentioned popular free-thought journals, *Ironclad Age* and *The Freethinkers' Magazine* (J.R. Monroe and H.L. Green, respectively), published a few pamphlets under their magazines' imprints. Nothing especially noteworthy issued from their presses, however. The American Secular Union published a few pamphlets relating to its own organization and a few items by Franklin Steiner.

Charles Watts, an important British freethinker, spent several years in Toronto, Canada, in the 1880s where he published a journal called *Secular Thought* (336). The Office of *Secular Thought* issued a number of pamphlets of Watts' writings. After Watts returned to England in 1891, J. Spencer Ellis took over *Secular Thought*. While *Secular Thought* was not an *American* freethought journal or pub-lisher, it is mentioned here because it was the *only* Canadian free-thought publisher and the major Canadian freethought journal.

Charles C. Moore founded a journal called *The Blue Grass Blade* (263) in Lexington, Kentucky. Moore's Blue Grass Printing Company also published a few pamphlets and several of Moore's own works. Another company that occasionally published freethought books, but cannot really be called a freethought publisher, was the Open Court Publishing Company in Illinois. It published *The Open Court* (328) magazine and *The Monist* (324). The first editor of *The Open Court* was B. F. Underwood, but Paul Carus soon took over. Most of the books issued by Open Court were either original works by Carus or reprints of philosophical articles in his magazines. Carus, who wanted to found a "religion of science," wrote *The History of the Devil and the Idea of Evil* (268).

* * *

A national conference of the Unitarian church was organized in 1865, and a period of rapid expansion and of aggressive denomina-tional life ensued. At the conference were members of the more liberal wing of the church—those who were not satisfied with the more con-servative Unitarian faction. A decisive encounter between Unitarian orthodoxy and the radicals did not take place, however until the first annual meeting of the National Conference of Unitarian Churches, held at Syracuse in 1866. The radical group held a series of meetings as a result of which the Free Religious Association was formed at a public meeting held on May 30, 1867. Octavius Brooks Frothingham (1822-1895) was chosen president; Robert Dale Owen, Thomas Wentworth Higginson, and Caroline M. Severance vice-presidents; and William J. Potter secretary. The activities of the Free Religious Asso-ciation were confined principally to New England, particularly to Boston.

Annual conferences were held, but the membership remained fairly small.

The Free Religious Association sponsored a magazine called *The Index* (309) published at Toledo, Ohio, from 1870 to 1872, and then at Boston. Francis Ellingwood Abbot (1836-1903) was editor until 1881, at which time William J. Potter and Benjamin F. Underwood succeeded. The association continued to be active and aggressive for about twenty-five years, after which it declined. The last meetings were held in 1923.

For an excellent history of the Free Religious Association, see *Free Religion: An American Faith* (330) by Stow Persons. Also see Chapter IV in *American Freethought, 1860-1914* (44) by Sidney Warren. Books on the religious beliefs of the association members include references 247, 248, 293, 294, 296, and 297. Biographical sketches of Francis Ellingwood Abbot, Octavius Brooks Frothingham, and William J. Potter are in the *Dictionary of American Biography* (79). Frothingham's *Recollections and Impressions, 1822-1890* (295) is autobiographical.

Felix Adler (1851-1933), a past president of the Free Religious Association, founded the Ethical Culture Society in New York City in 1876. This society was non-theistic in emphasis, believing in "deed, not creed" and in "a society which shall be practical as well as spiritual and unhampered by sectarian religious dogma." Other societies were founded in Chicago in 1885 and in St. Louis in 1886.

Ethical Culture societies held regular public meetings closely resembling church services, with music, periods of quiet meditation, the reading of Scripture or inspired prose or poetry, and an address by the leader upon a pertinent social, political, philosophical, ethical, or religious theme. The American Ethical Union, founded in 1889, was a federation of Ethical Culture societies and fellowships in the United States. More will be said about Ethical Culture societies in the next chapter.

The best book on the history of Ethical Culture societies is *Toward Common Ground* (331) by Howard B. Radest. Books by Felix Adler which are helpful in understanding the Ethical Culture movement include references 249, 250, and 251. See also *The Fiftieth Anniversary of the Ethical Movement, 1876-1926* (253), which was edited by the American Ethical Union.

Mangasar Murgurditch Mangasarian (1859-1943), born and educated in Turkey, attended Princeton Theological Seminary and became a Presbyterian minister. He abandoned Presbyterian doctrine after reading Emerson and Theodore Parker; he became associated with the New York Ethical Society in 1889 and with the Chicago Ethical Society in 1897. In 1900, he founded the Independent Religious Society in Chicago, for which he was lecturer until he retired in 1925. He was the author of *The Neglected Book* (322), which was also published under the title *The Bible Unveiled* by the Independent Religious Society, and *A New Catechism* (323).

BIBLIOGRAPHY

247. Abbot, Francis Ellingwood. *Scientific Theism.* Boston: Little Brown & Co., 1885.

248. Abbot, Francis Ellingwood. *The Way Out of Agnosticism.* Boston: Little, Brown & Co., 1889.

249. Adler, Felix. *An Ethical Philosophy of Life.* New York: D. Appleton & Co., 1918.

250. Adler, Felix. *Creed and Deed.* New York: G. P. Putnam's Sons, 1877.

251. Adler, Felix. *The Religion of Duty.* New York: McClure, 1905.

252. Amberley, John Russell, Viscount. *An Analysis of Religious Belief.* New York: D. M. Bennett, 1878. British edition published in London by Trübner & Co. in 1876.

253. American Ethical Union, ed. *The Fiftieth Anniversary of the Ethical Movement, 1876-1926.* New York: D. Appleton & Co., 1926.

254. Anderson, David D. *Robert Ingersoll.* New York: Twayne Publishers, 1972.

255. Baker, I. Newton. *An Intimate View of Robert G. Ingersoll.* New York: C. P. Farrell, 1920.

256. Bell, W. S. *A Handbook of Freethought.* San Francisco: W. S. Bell, 1890. Later sold by the Truth Seeker Co.

257. Bennett, D. M. *The Champions of the Church.* New York: D. M. Bennett, 1879.

258. Bennett, D. M., and Humphrey, G. H. *Christianity and Infidelity: The Humphrey-Bennett Discussion.* New York: D. M. Bennett, 1879.

259. Bennett, D. M. *Thirty Discussions, Bible Stories, Essays and Lectures.* New York: D. M. Bennett, 1879.

260. Bennett, D. M. *A Truth Seeker Around the World.* New York: D. M. Bennett, 1882, 4 vols.

261. Bennett, D. M., ed. *Truth Seeker Tracts Upon a Variety*

of Subjects. New York: D. M. Bennett, various dates (1870s), 3 vols.

262. Berman, Milton. *John Fiske: The Evolution of a Popularizer.* Cambridge, Mass.: Harvard University Press, 1961.

263. *Blue Grass Blade, The,* a weekly freethought periodical (although often published irregularly) from 1884 to the early 1900s in Lexington, Kentucky, and Cincinnati by Charles C. Moore. Moore published his autobiography *Behind the Bars: 31498* in 1899 (Lexington, Ky.: Blue Grass Printing Co.).

264. Bradlaugh, Charles. *A Few Words About the Devil and Other Essays and Lectures.* New York: C. P. Somerby, n.d. (c. 1872).

265. [Bradlaugh, Charles] as "Iconoclast," Johnson, W. H., and Watts, Charles. *Half-Hours with the Freethinkers.* Boston: J.P. Mendum, 1877. Original edition published in London by Austin & Co., 1857.

266. Briggs, Austin, Jr. *The Novels of Harold Frederic.* Ithaca, N.Y.: Cornell University Press, 1969.

267. [Burr, William Henry]. *Revelations of Antichrist.* New York: D. M. Bennett; Boston: J. P. Mendum, 1879 (dual imprint).

268. Carus, Paul. *The History of the Devil and the Idea of Evil from the Earliest Times to the Present Day.* Chicago: Open Court Publishing Co., 1900.

269. [Cassels, Walter R.]. *Supernatural Religion.* New York: D. M. Bennett, 1879. Original edition published in London by Longmans, Green & Co. in 1874 (2 vols.), with a third volume from the same publisher in 1877.

270. Chugerman, Samuel. *Lester F. Ward: The American Aristotle.* Durham, N.C.: Duke University Press, 1939.

271. Clemens, Samuel L. (as "Mark Twain"). *Christian Science.* New York: Harper & Brothers, 1907.

272. Clemens, Samuel L. *Letters from the Earth.* New York: Harper & Row, 1962.

273. Clemens, Samuel L. *The Mysterious Stranger.* New York: Harper & Brothers, 1916.

274. Clemens, Samuel L. *Report from Paradise.* New York: Harper & Brothers, 1952.

275. Clemens, Samuel L. *What Is Man?* New York: DeVinne Press, 1906.

276. Cooper, Robert. *The Immortality of the Soul, Religiously and Philosophically Considered.* Boston: J. P. Mendum, 1882. Originally published in London by J. Watson in 1852.

277. Cooper, Robert. *The Infidel's Text-Book: Being the Substance of Thirteen Lectures on the Bible.* Boston: J. P. Mendum, 1858.

278. Cramer, Clarence H. *Royal Bob.* Indianapolis: Bobbs-Merrill Co., 1952.

279. Deland, Margaret. *John Ward, Preacher.* Boston: Houghton Mifflin Co., 1888.

280. Dibble, R. F. "The Devil's Advocate." *The American Mercury* 3 (1924):64-70.

281. Doane, Thomas W. *Bible Myths and Their Parallels in Other Religions.* New York: Truth Seeker Co., 1882.

282. Draper, John W. *History of the Conflict Between Religion and Science.* New York: D. Appleton & Co., 1874.

283. Ensor, Allison. *Mark Twain & the Bible.* Lexington, Ky.: University of Kentucky Press, 1969.

284. Fawcett, Edgar. *Agnosticism and Other Essays.* Chicago: Belford, Clarke & Co., 1889.

285. Feuerbach, Ludwig A. *The Essence of Christianity.* New York: A. K. Butts & Co., 1873. First published in German (Leipzig, Germany: O. Wigand, 1849). First American edition was New York: C. Blanchard, 1857. Also called *The Essence of Religion* in some editions.

286. Fiske, John. *Outlines of Cosmic Philosophy.* Boston: Houghton Mifflin Co., 1874.

287. Fleming, Donald. *John W. Draper.* Philadelphia: University of Pennsylvania Press, 1950.

288. Foner, Philip S. *Mark Twain, Social Critic.* New York: International Publishers, 1958.

289. Frederic, Harold. *The Damnation of Theron Ware.* New York: Hurst & Co., 1896.

290. *Freethinkers' Magazine, The,* a monthly freethought periodical published at Buffalo by H. L. Green, 1882-1894. See also no. 292 for the subsequent publishing history of this periodical.

291. *Freethought,* a weekly freethought periodical published at San Francisco by George E. Macdonald and Samuel P. Putnam, 1888-1891.

292. *Freethought Magazine,* a monthly freethought periodical published at Chicago by H. L. Green, 1895-1903. A continuation of *The Freethinkers' Magazine* (see no. 290).

293. Frothingham, Octavius Brooks. *Beliefs of the Unbelievers.* New York: G. P. Putnam's Sons, 1876.

294. Frothingham, Octavius Brooks, and Adler, Felix. *The Radical Pulpit.* New York: D. M. Bennett, 1877.

295. Frothingham, Octavius Brooks. *Recollections and Impressions, 1822-1890.* New York: G. P. Putnam's Sons, 1891.

296. Frothingham, Octavius Brooks. *The Religion of Humanity.* New York: G. P. Putnam's Sons, 1877.

297. Frothingham, Octavius Brooks. *The Safest Creed, and Twelve Other Recent Discourses on Religion.* New York: A. K. Butts & Co., 1874.

298. Gage, Matilda Joslyn. *Woman, Church and State: A Historical Account of Woman Through the Christian Ages, With Reminiscences of the Matriarchate.* New York: Truth Seeker Co., 1893.

299. Gardener, Helen Hamilton. *Men, Women and Gods, and Other Lectures.* New York: Truth Seeker Co., 1885.

300. Geismar, Maxwell, ed. *Mark Twain and the Three R's, Race, Religion, Revolution and Related Matters.* New York: Bobbs-Merrill Co., 1973.

301. Gorham, Charles T. *Robert G. Ingersoll.* London: Watts & Co., 1921. Abridged American edition published by E. Haldeman-Julius at Girard, Kansas, 1947.

302. Graves, Kersey. *The World's Sixteen Crucified Saviors.* Boston: Colby & Rich, 1874. Many subsequent editions published by the Truth Seeker Company.

303. Harnsberger, Caroline Thomas. *Mark Twain's Views of Religion.* Evanston, Ill.: Schori Press, 1961.

304. Harrison, Stanley R. *Edgar Fawcett.* New York: Twayne Publishers, 1972.

305. Hirsch, William. *Religion and Civilization.* New York: Truth Seeker Co., 1912.

306. Holbach, Paul Henri Thiry, Baron D'. *Letters to Eugenia.* Boston: J. P. Mendum, 1857. First English translation published by R. Carlile in London in 1819.

307. *Iconoclast, The,* a monthly freethought periodical published at Washington, D.C., by Lester Frank Ward, March 1870-August 1871.

308. *Independent Pulpit, The,* a monthly freethought periodical published at Waco, Texas, by J. D. Shaw, 1882-1901. The name was changed to *The Searchlight* in 1902 (see no. 335).

309. *Index, The,* a weekly freethought periodical devoted to Free Religion. It was published at Toledo, Ohio, 1870-1872, and then at Boston, 1873-1886. The "Nine Demands of Liberalism" were first published in this periodical on April 6, 1872.

310. Ingersoll, Robert G. *The Gods and Other Lectures.* Peoria, Ill.: C. P. Farrell, 1874.

311. Ingersoll, Robert G. *The Works of Robert G. Ingersoll.* New York: C. P. Farrell, 1900, 12 vols. The so-called Dresden Edition.

Subsequent reprintings in 1902, 1909-1911 (at which time a thirteenth volume containing Herman Kittridge's biography of Ingersoll [see no. 314] was added to the set), 1912, and 1915. A cheaper red binding and smaller page size were used on reprintings in 1929, 1930, and 1933.

312. *Ironclad Age, The,* a weekly agnostic periodical published at Indianapolis by J. R. Monroe, 1881-1898. Upon Monroe's death in 1891, it was published by his daughter, and upon her death in 1895, by P. H. and Pearl A. Powers.

313. Keeler, Bronson. *A Short History of the Bible.* New York: C. P. Farrell, 1909.

314. Kittredge, Herman. *Ingersoll: A Biographical Appreciation.* New York: Dresden Publishing Co., 1911.

315. Larson, Orvin. *American Infidel: Robert G. Ingersoll.* New York: Citadel Press, 1962. Perhaps the best biography of Ingersoll. Contains an excellent bibliography.

316. Lewis, Arthur M. *The Struggle Between Science and Superstition.* Chicago: Charles H. Kerr & Co., 1934.

317. Lewis, Joseph. *Ingersoll the Magnificent.* New York: Freethought Press Association, 1957.

318. *Liberal, The,* a freethought periodical published in Liberal, Missouri, by George H. Walser, 1881-1889. There were several other freethought periodicals with this name (see the next chapter).

319. *Liberal Review, The,* a freethought periodical formed by the merging of *Freethought Magazine* and *The Torch of Reason.* Published in Chicago and edited by Thaddeus B. Wakeman and M. M. Mangasarian from 1904 to 1906 + 1918.

320. Macdonald, Eugene M. *Col. Robert G. Ingersoll As He Is.* New York: Truth Seeker Co., n.d. (circa 1885). After 1899 (when Ingersoll died), this book was republished with the new title *Col. Robert G. Ingersoll As He Was.*

321. *Man,* a freethought periodical published by the Board of Managers of the National Liberal League and edited by Thaddeus B. Wakeman, 1878-1884, in New York.

322. Mangasarian, M. M. *The Neglected Book.* New York: Truth Seeker Co., 1926. Also published under the title *The Bible Unveiled* by the Independent Religious Society in Chicago.

323. Mangasarian, M. M. *A New Catechism.* Chicago: Independent Religious Society, 1913.

324. *Monist, The,* a quarterly magazine devoted to the philosophy of science and published at Chicago by the Open Court Publishing Co., 1890-1936.

325. Moore, James P. *This Strange Town—Liberal, Missouri.* Liberal, Mo.: Liberal News, 1963.

326. Neider, Charles, ed. "Mark Twain—Reflections on Religion." *The Hudson Review* 16 (1963):329-352.

327. O'Donnell, Thomas F., and Franchere, Hoyt G. *Harold Frederic.* New York: Twayne Publishers, 1961.

328. *Open Court, The,* a liberal periodical which was in many respects the successor to *The Index* (see no. 309). Published at Chicago as a monthly, 1887-1933 and as a quarterly, 1934-1936. Paul Carus was the editor for most of its life, and B. F. Underwood its first editor.

329. Pannill, H. Burrell. *The Religion of John Fiske.* Durham, N.C.: Duke University Press, 1957.

330. Persons, Stow. *Free Religion: An American Faith.* New Haven: Yale University Press, 1947.

331. Radest, Howard B. *Toward Common Ground: The Story of the Ethical Societies in the United States.* New York: Frederick Ungar Publishing Co., 1969.

332. Reade, W. Winwood. *The Martyrdom of Man.* New York: A. K. Butts & Co., 1874. First published in London by Trübner & Co., 1872.

333. Remsburg, John E. *The Bible.* New York: Truth Seeker Co., 1907.

334. Remsburg, John E. *The Christ.* New York: Truth Seeker Co., 1909.

335. *Searchlight, The,* a monthly freethought periodical published at Waco, Texas, by J. D. Shaw, 1902-1910. Called *The Independent Pulpit* (see no. 308) prior to 1902.

336. *Secular Thought,* a freethought periodical published at Toronto, Canada. Edited by Charles Watts from 1884 to 1891 and by J. Spencer Ellis from 1891 to 1919.

337. Simpson, James Young. *Landmarks in the Struggle Between Science and Religion.* New York: George H. Doran Co., 1926.

338. Smith, Edward Garstin. *The Life and Remniscences of Robert G. Ingersoll.* New York: National Weekly Publishing Co., 1904.

339. Smith, James Ward, and Jamison, A. Leland, eds. *Religious Perspectives in American Culture,* vol. 2. Princeton, N.J.: Princeton University Press, 1961.

340. Taylor, Robert. *The Devil's Pulpit.* Boston: J. P. Mendum, 1873. The first half of the original British publication of this title. J. P. Mendum published the second half in 1857 under the title *The Astronomico-Theological Lectures.* Original edition published in London by Richard Carlile in weekly numbers from 1831 to 1832.

341. Taylor, Robert. *Syntagma of the Evidences of the Christian Religion.* Boston: J. P. Mendum, 1865. Originally published in London by Richard Carlile in 1828.

342. *Torch of Reason, The,* a freethought periodical published at Silverton, Oregon, and Kansas City, Missouri, 1896-1903. Thaddeus B. Wakeman served as the editor during most of its lifetime.

343. *Truth Seeker, The,* a freethought periodical published weekly in Paris, Illinois, 1873-1874, and in New York City, 1874-1929; as a monthly in New York City, 1930-1964, and in San Diego, 1964-present. Successive editors have been D. M. Bennett, Eugene M. Macdonald, George E. Macdonald, Charles Smith, and James Hervey Johnson.

344. Underwood, Sara. *Heroines of Freethought.* New York: C. P. Somerby, 1876.

345. Wakefield, Eva Ingersoll, ed. *The Letters of Robert G. Ingersoll.* New York: Philosophical Library, 1951.

346. White, Andrew Dickson. *The Autobiography of Andrew Dickson White.* New York: The Century Co., 1905, 2 vols.

347. White, Andrew Dickson. *A History of the Warfare of Science with Theology in Christendom.* New York: D. Appleton & Co., 1896, 2 vols.

348. White, Edward A. *Science and Religion in American Thought.* Palo Alto, Calif.: Stanford University Press, 1952.

349. Winston, George P. *John Fiske.* New York: Twayne Publishers, 1972.

350. Writers' Program. *Missouri, A Guide to the "Show Me" State.* New York: Duell, Sloan & Pierce, 1941. One of the American Guide Series.

4.

★ ★ ★ ★ ★ ★ ★ ★ ★

Freethought in the Twentieth Century

No one has yet written the history of freethought in the twentieth century up to the present time. *American Freethought, 1860-1914* (44) by Sidney Warren covers the very beginning of the period, and *Fifty Years of Freethought* (23) by George E. Macdonald covers the first quarter of the century.

The leading personalities of the freethought movement during the twentieth century include Clarence Darrow, Maynard Shipley, Joseph Lewis, George E. Macdonald, Charles L. Smith, Woolsey Teller, Marshall Gauvin, Franklin Steiner, Emanuel Haldeman-Julius, Bernard Rocca, Paul Blanshard, Joseph Wheless, Henry M. Tichenor, and Madalyn Murray O'Hair.

Perhaps the most distinguished freethinker of this period was Clarence Seward Darrow (1857-1938). Born in Kinsman, Ohio, the son of a freethinking father, he moved to Chicago where he spent the remainder of his life.

Darrow became the most famous criminal lawyer of his time. Undoubtedly the most widely publicized of Darrow's cases was the Scopes evolution trial in Dayton, Tennessee, in 1925, a trial of particular interest to freethinkers. Darrow was the main lawyer for the defense, and William Jennings Bryan for the prosecution. Worldwide publicity was given to the trial, which was a classic example of the confrontation between science and religion. Books written about this trial include references 352, 391, 410, 411, 506, 509, and 532.

The Tennessee law on the teaching of evolution was repealed by the Tennessee legislature in 1967, and in 1968 the United States Supreme Court declared the Arkansas law on the teaching of evolution to be unconstitutional. *Inherit the Wind* (442), a play by Jerome Lawrence and Robert E. Lee was based on the Scopes trial and was later made into a motion picture.

Throughout his life, Clarence Darrow remained an agnostic. The best explication of his religious beliefs or disbeliefs is given in his autobiography, *The Story of My Life* (390). See particularly Chapter 42, "Questions Without Answers," Chapter 43, "Future Life," and Chapter 44, "Delusion of Design and Progress." Several biographies have been written about Darrow, including those in references 416, 474, 521, and 538.

Maynard Shipley (1872-1934), in his book *The War on Modern Science* (510), tells of the efforts various states have made to ban the teaching of the theory of evolution. Shipley, a self-educated scientist, was president of the Science League of America. His wife, Miriam Allen DeFord Shipley, has written a biography of him entitled *Up-Hill All the Way* (392).

Another book that should be mentioned here is Oscar Riddle's *The Unleashing of Evolutionary Thought* (493), a brilliant account of the conflict between science and religion.

Joseph Lewis (1889-1968), one of the most active freethinkers of the twentieth century, was born in Montgomery, Alabama, the son of a Jewish merchant. He came to New York City during the 1920s. In 1925 he was elected president of the Freethinkers of America, an organization founded in 1915 and incorporated in 1925, and remained president for life. In fact, he virtually *was* the organization. Through his writings, lecturing, and lawsuits, he fought for the complete separation of church and state. His freethought views can be studied in references 112, 317, 447, 448, 449, 450, and 451.

Lewis also edited a monthly magazine entitled *The Age of Reason* (351). There is a so-called biography of Lewis entitled *Joseph Lewis: Enemy of God* (419) by Arthur H. Howland, but it consists mostly of quotations from his writings. Lewis appears in *Who's Who in America* (541).

George Everett Macdonald (1857-1944) succeeded his brother as editor of *The Truth Seeker* (343) in 1909. During his editorship (1909-1937), *The Truth Seeker* was the leading freethought magazine in the United States. The magazine had been a weekly during most of its history, but in 1930 it became a monthly. Macdonald became editor emeritus in 1937 and continued in this capacity, as well as a writer for the magazine, until his death in 1944. He was active in the American Secular Union and was the author of *A Short History of the Inquisition* (460) and *Fifty Years of Freethought* (23). There is a biographical sketch of Macdonald in references 24 and 30.

Charles L. Smith (1887-1964) became the fourth editor of *The Truth Seeker* in 1937. Born in Arkansas, he became active in freethought circles in New York following his service in World War I, his attendance at Harvard, and his study for the ministry. Smith was president of the American Association for the Advancement of Atheism for many years, and he also served as president of the National Liberal League. In 1964, upon Smith's death, James Hervey Johnson, author of *Superior Men* (429), became editor of *The Truth Seeker*. Smith's freethought views can be studied in *Sensism: The Philosophy of the West* (512). For more information on Smith, see two magazine articles in *World's Work* (385 and 386) by Homer Croy.

Woolsey Teller (1890-1954) was associate editor of *The Truth Seeker* from 1936 until his death in 1954. He had been active as a freethinker through lectures, debates, and writings since 1908. His best known work was *Essays of an Atheist* (526); he also wrote *The Atheism of Astronomy* (525). Teller, along with Charles Smith and Freeman Hopwood, founded the American Association for the Advancement of Atheism in 1925.

Marshall Gauvin (1881-   ) was born in Moncton, New Brunswick, Canada, the son of a Baptist father and a Roman Catholic mother. Through wide reading, he became a freethinker. At the age of twenty, he became a freethought lecturer in New Brunswick and Nova Scotia. Gauvin came to the United States in 1912 to pursue his career as a freethought lecturer. He was engaged by the Pittsburgh Rationalist Society as their lecturer and remained there from 1914 until 1920. He then went to Minneapolis, lecturing there until 1926. During his stay in these two cities, he traveled widely, giving lectures on freethought. In 1926, he went to Winnipeg, Canada. He is now retired and was still living in Winnipeg at last report. Gauvin has contributed innumerable articles to *The Truth Seeker* (343) and has been its assistant editor for many years. He is the author of *Fundamentals of Freethought* (409) and of a number of pamphlets and debates. For an autobiographical sketch, see the March 1975 issue of *The Truth Seeker* (343).

Franklin Steiner (1872-1945), a freethought lecturer and writer, was a vice-president of the American Secular Union, secretary of the American Rationalist Association during its existence, and the principal force behind that organization for many years. He contributed to *The Boston Investigator* (177) and to *The Truth Seeker* (343). He wrote *The Religious Beliefs of Our Presidents* (40) and *Religion and Roguery* (517). For a biographical sketch, see references 24 and 30.

Emanuel Haldeman-Julius (1889-1951), a newspaperman turned publisher, was born in Philadelphia and spent his early life as a writer and reporter, mostly on socialist newspapers. He became a free-

thinker from reading the works of Thomas Paine and Robert G. Ingersoll. In 1915, Julius received a call to come out to Girard, Kansas,
to help run *The Appeal to Reason,* a socialist newspaper which at that
time was a powerful weekly with a large circulation. Julius married
Marcet Haldeman, an actress who had returned to her home in Girard
after her parents' deaths, to run the family bank; they joined and hy-
phenated their last names to Haldeman-Julius. In 1919, Haldeman-Julius
bought the newspaper from his previous boss and on an experimental
basis began reprinting classics of literature in small, cheap pamphlets
on his newspaper presses. This was the start of the Little Blue Books
that were to revolutionize American publishing. (These are discussed
in detail later in this chapter.)

Bernard Thompson Rocca, Sr. (1894-   ), was quite active in
the freethought movement from 1950 to the 1970s. He was president of the United Secularists of America, which sponsors the magazine *Progressive World* (489). He authored the following freethought
books: *Fitting in the Pieces* (500) and *Faith, Fact and Reason,* Volume
1 (498) and Volume 2 (499).

Paul Blanshard (1892-   ) trained as a Congregational minister
and for a short time served as pastor of a Tampa, Florida, church. His
liberal thinking eventually led him to resign the pulpit, after which
he went to law school and became an authority on church and state
relations. Blanshard has written extensively in the field of religious
controversy, particularly in church and state relations. Some of his
books are cited in references 365, 366, 367, 368, 369, 370, 371,
and 372.

Joseph Wheless (1868-1950), author, judge, and specialist in
Latin American law, was an active supporter of the freethought movement. He was an attorney for the Freethinkers of America, the American Association for the Advancement of Atheism, and the New York
League for the Separation of Church and State. He wrote *Is It God's
Word?* (540) and *Forgery in Christianity* (539) in both of which he
questions the authenticity of the Bible and Christian history. A biographical sketch is in the *National Cyclopedia of American Biography*
(473); he has also appeared in *Who's Who in America* (541).

Henry Mulford Tichenor (1858-1922) was an editor who often
wrote on freethought subjects. He was a socialist and the editor of
The Melting Pot, a socialist magazine published in St. Louis. He wrote
The Life and Exploits of Jehovah (529), which was a satire on the
Jewish God; *The Sorceries and Scandals of Satan* (530); and *Tales
of Theology* (531). A biographical sketch of Tichenor appears in the
National Cyclopedia of Biography (473).

Madalyn Murray O'Hair (1919-   ) first gained national attention in 1962-1963 through her legal fight over Bible reading in the Baltimore, Maryland, public school system. This fight culminated in a Supreme Court decision stating that enforced Bible reading in the public schools was in violation of the First Amendment of the Constitution. O'Hair is an atheist and promotes her views through lectures, television appearances, magazines, and her organization, the Society of Separationists (recently renamed American Atheists). She lives in Austin, Texas, which is the headquarters for her activities. By training, O'Hair is an attorney and social worker. She frequently uses her legal training to help file law suits on matters involving the separation of church and state. She publishes a newsletter intended only for members, as well as *The American Atheist* (354).

Information concerning O'Hair has appeared in many newspapers and magazines. See "The Most Hated Woman in America" (418) by Jane Howard in *Life* and "Mrs. Murray's War on God" (454) by Robert Liston in *The Saturday Evening Post.* An interview with O'Hair appeared in the October 1965 issue of *Playboy* magazine. She has authored the following books: *What on Earth Is an Atheist!* (478), *An Atheist Epic: Bill Murray and the Baltimore Board of Education* (476), and *Freedom Under Siege* (477).

Although not directly connected with the freethought movement, Luther Burbank (1849-1926), the great plant wizard, was a freethinker. He delivered an address in the First Congregational Church in San Francisco in 1926, in which he said: "I reiterate: The religion of most people is what they would like to believe, not what they do believe, and very few stop to examine its foundation underneath. The idea that a good God would send people to a burning hell is utterly damnable to me. . . . I don't want to have anything to do with such a God. I am a lover of man and of Christ as a man and his work, . . . but nevertheless, just as he was an infidel then, I am an infidel to-day. I . . . claim the right to worship the infinite, everlasting, almighty God of this vast universe as revealed to us . . . by demonstrable truths of our savior, science." This address created quite a stir in the religious world. It is included in *Luther Burbank, "Our Beloved Infidel"* (383) by Frederick W. Clampett. This volume also contains a general discussion of Burbank's religious views.

William John Fielding (1886-1973), who was essentially a self-educated man, wrote more than thirty Little Blue Books for E. Haldeman-Julius, as well as a number of full-sized volumes for other publishers. The freethought classic he authored was *The Shackles of the Supernatural* (399). There is a biographical sketch of Fielding in *Who's*

Who in America (541). His autobiography is entitled *All the Lives I Have Lived* (398).

Theodore Schroeder (1864-1953) was an attorney who heavily involved himself in freedom of the press, free speech, and religious liberty cases. Himself a freethinker, he was a friend and attorney to many of the leading freethinkers of the 1900-1945 period. In early life, Schroeder was influenced by Robert G. Ingersoll and Ludwig Feuerbach's writings. He founded the Free Speech League in 1911. He defended Moses Harman in 1906, the anti-Catholic periodical *The Menace* on the issue of freedom of the press in 1915, and Michael Mockus on a blasphemy charge in 1916. He also defended Bishop William Montgomery Brown on a charge of heresy in 1924. Schroeder wrote several books, mostly on obscenity laws and on freedom of the press and free speech. His only book which could fit in a freethought classification was his 1919 brief in the blasphemy trial of Mockus, which is really a history of prosecutions for "offenses against religion," including blasphemy charges. This book, published by his own Free Speech League in New York in 1919, was *Constitutional Free Speech Defined and Defended in an Unfinished Argument in a Case of Blasphemy.* Schroeder also wrote several articles on blasphemy trials for *The Truth Seeker* (343).

Thomas Alva Edison (1847-1931), the great inventor, was also a freethinker. He was a subscriber to *The Truth Seeker* (343) and supported the freethought cause financially. For Edison's religious views, see *Edison: A Biography* (430) by Matthew Josephson and "Thomas A. Edison on Immortality" (397) by Marshall Edward in *The Columbian Magazine.*

Henry Louis Mencken (1880-1956), although not an actual member of the freethought movement, expressed his rationalist views in many of his writings, particularly in *A Treatise on the Gods* (468) which was one of his most popular books. His atheistic views are also expressed in a letter written to Will Durant in 1933 published in *A Treasury of the World's Greatest Letters* (505), edited by M. Lincoln Schuster. Several biographies have been written about Mencken, including those cited in references 373, 431, 465, and 518.

* * *

The American Secular Union, whose origin goes back to 1876, continued into the twentieth century but with less vitality than before. It held congresses in 1901-1904, 1910, 1911, 1916, and 1920; after 1920, a Board of Directors met annually and elected officers. Eugene M. Macdonald served as president from 1900 until 1909, and John E. Remsburg from 1916 until his death in 1919. The organization ceased to function after the 1920s. Further information on the American Secular Union can be found in *Fifty Years of Freethought* (23) and in the Golden Jubilee Issue of *The Truth Seeker* (September 1, 1923).

In 1924, the American Rationalist Association was organized. Percy Ward was elected president and served three years. Its secretary, Franklin Steiner, was the principal force behind the organization during its existence. It died during the 1930s.

The Freethinkers of America was one of the most active freethought organizations during this period. Joseph Lewis was the president during most of its lifetime, serving from 1925 until his death in 1968. Martin J. Martin made an attempt to revive the organization, but had rather limited success.

In 1925, the American Association for the Advancement of Atheism was founded with the purposes of carrying on the work of Thomas Paine, Voltaire, and Robert G. Ingersoll, and of opposing the teaching of religion in the public schools. The association (called "The 4 As" by members) reached a membership of 8,700 in 1931, but since then its membership has declined. Charles Smith was president of the organization during most of its history. After the 1930s, when the association had achieved widespread magazine and newspaper publicity, it became relatively inactive. In the 1960s, James Hervey Johnson tried rather unsuccessfully to revive the organization. Recently, its name was changed to the Atheist Association.

In 1930, George B. Vetter and Martin Green of New York University, through the use of 600 questionnaires, made a study of factors that had caused members of the American Association for the Advancement of Atheism, to become atheists. The result of the study, entitled "Personality and Group Factors in the Making of Atheists" (536), appeared in the *Journal of Abnormal and Social Psychology*.

The National Liberal League (not connected with the earlier organization of the same name) was founded in New York in 1945 for the purpose of maintaining the separation of church and state. It was also interested in saving public schools from church control, and it sought the repeal of all laws based upon religious beliefs, particularly those restricting the rights of unbelievers. The league's membership totaled 2,450 in 1947, but decreased after that time. It gradually faded from view in the 1950s. However, the National Liberal League was reactivated in 1965 by James Hervey Johnson, editor of the *Truth Seeker* (343) with the name changed to National Liberal League for Separation of Church and State. Johnson is president. It has seventy members and meets annually.

The American Rationalist Federation was organized in St. Louis in 1954 for those who subscribe to the philosophy of rationalism. It still holds annual conventions, which are usually held in Chicago or St. Louis. It also has an annual award for the "Rationalist of the Year." The federation publishes *The American Rationalist* magazine (356).

The United Secularists of America was founded by William McCarthy in New Jersey in 1947. Its primary activity was the publication of the magazine *Progressive World* (489). As noted earlier, Bernard T. Rocca, Sr., was president of this organization for many years.

Other freethought organizations that are active today, or at least were so until recently, include the Society of Separationists (and American Atheists) of Austin, Texas, the Twin City Secularists (St. Paul, Minnesota), the Freethinkers of Southern California, the Rationalist Society of St. Louis, and the Northern California Secular Society (San Francisco).

* * *

During the twentieth century, *The Truth Seeker* (343) continued to be the leading freethought magazine, at least until midcentury. The successive editors during the twentieth century were Eugene M. Macdonald, George E. Macdonald, Charles Smith, and James Hervey Johnson. In the early 1930s, George E. Macdonald contemplated suspending the magazine, but instead changed it from a weekly to a monthly; it has continued as a monthly since then. In 1900, the circulation was 7,000, but it decreased to about 2,000 in 1933. The circulation today is only about 700, largely because it now supports a mixture of racism and atheism.

The Age of Reason (351), a magazine edited by Joseph Lewis, president of the Freethinkers of America, was published from 1937 until Lewis's death in 1968. During this period, it went through a series of name changes (it was first called *The Bulletin of the Freethinkers of America,* then *Common Sense,* then *The Freethinker,* and finally *The Age of Reason*). Its highest circulation was about 4,000.

The Arbitrator (357) was a magazine published in New York City from 1918 to 1943 whose stated purpose was to outlaw war, abolish poverty, unveil superstition, and secure justice. During most of its life, it was edited by William Floyd.

Progressive World (489), a freethought magazine sponsored by the United Secularists of America, began publication in 1947 and is still published. Initially issued from Clifton, New Jersey, it moved to Los Angeles and then to San Francisco. Its first editor was Lowell H. Choate. During most of its existence, the magazine was edited by

Hugh Robert Orr (1887-1967). Upon his death, his wife Frances Orr became the editor; she was succeeded by Catherine Sears, who served from 1971 to 1973. Since that time, Sydney A. Zucker has been editor. *Progressive World* was a monthly magazine until 1974 when it became a bimonthly publication. It currently has a circulation of about 1,200.

The *American Rationalist* (356) published by the American Rationalist Association, began in St. Louis in 1956. The magazine was a monthly until 1966, at which time it became a bimonthly. Its successive editors have been Arthur B. Hewson, Lowell H. Choate, Edd Doerr, Walter Hoops, and Paul Kaufmann. It has a circulation of slightly less than 1,000.

Other freethought magazines published currently, or during the twentieth century (some of which existed for only a short time), include *The American Atheist* (354), *The Atheist* (359), *Common Herd* (384), *The Crucible* (387), *The Crucible* (388), *The Free Humanist* (405), *Freethought Opinion* (406), *Humanitarian Review* (426), *Ingersoll Memorial Beacon* (427), *The Liberal* (453), *The Militant Atheist* (469), *The Open Mind* (479), *Progressive Forum* (488), *Queen Silver's Magazine* (490), *The Rationalist* (491), and *The Ripsaw* (494).

The above periodicals were the principal freethought magazines in English (American foreign language periodicals are covered in Appendix I) of the twentieth century. Other magazines were for the most part local and existed only a short time, or were mainly mimeographed. Included among these are *The Quester, Secular Subjects* (started in 1948), *The Lookout, The Volcano, Exit, Repartee, The Secularist, SEA Journal, Appeal to Reason, The South-West Freethinkers' News, The American Freethinker, Atomic Era, The Philosopher, Heuristic,* and *The New Perspective.* (The Haldeman-Julius periodical publications are discussed below.)

In 1972, Arno Press of New York published *Atheist Magazines: A Sampling, 1927-70* (360). This volume contains copies of ten freethought magazines published between 1927 and 1970, but the period chosen is not representative of the high point in freethought publishing.

The novel *Elmer Gantry* (452) by Sinclair Lewis (1884-1951) is the story of a hypocritical Baptist minister who, after reading Ingersoll's works, no longer believed in his religion and was a sensational best seller in its day. It was later made into a motion picture. Biographies of Sinclair Lewis are cited in references 412, 475, 504, and 535.

A number of books with a freethought point of view have been published during the twentieth century. Since not enough time has passed to allow us to judge the relative importance of these works, the following list of references is rather unselective: 358, 361, 362, 364, 375, 376, 377, 379, 380, 381, 389, 393, 404, 408, 415, 417, 420, 421, 422, 423, 438, 443, 444, 445, 446, 457, 458, 461, 462, 463, 464, 497, 501, 502, 503, 507, 511, 514, 515, 537, and 542. In addition, the books cited in 466, 467, 508, and 514 treat specifically or in great detail the question of the existence of God.

* * *

In the twentieth century, several new freethought publishers appeared on the scene, but only two—E. Haldeman-Julius and Joseph Lewis, with his Freethought Press Association—can be considered major.

Soon after newspaperman Julius bought *The Appeal to Reason* in Girard, Kansas, in 1918, he began using its presses to also issue what came to be called Little Blue Books. These were paperbound pamphlets that sold at prices starting at 25 cents, but dipping later to as low as 5 cents each. At first, the booklets were mostly reprints of literary classics, but eventually the works of Paine, Voltaire, and Ingersoll were added. Soon, a whole section of booklets called "Freethought" was added. Eventually a number of larger pamphlets called Big Blue Books were added.

Around 1929, Joseph McCabe (1867-1955), a well-known British freethinker and ex-priest, was recruited to write Big and Little Blue Books. From 1929 to 1951 (when Haldeman-Julius died), McCabe wrote about 200 Little Blue Books and about 100 Big Blue Books. Most were on freethought subjects, although some were straight history, biography or "sexology."

Eventually, Haldeman-Julius sold over 400 million Little Blue Books, many of which he wrote himself. Because of the large number of titles published (over 3,000), no complete or inclusive list of freethought items can be readily given. Most of the titles were either classics by Ingersoll or Paine, or were based on articles that had been written for one of Haldeman-Julius's many magazines. Most of Joseph McCabe's publications started out this way—as articles.

Among the magazines Haldeman-Julius published (and which had at least some freethought content) were *The American Freeman* (a weekly newspaper), *The Haldeman-Julius Monthly* (later called *The Debunker*), *The Haldeman-Julius Quarterly*, *The Joseph McCabe Magazine, The Critic and Guide,* and *The Militant Atheist* (469).

Haldeman-Julius himself wrote many articles that were later issued as booklets, many of them on freethought subjects.

Several biographies of E. Haldeman-Julius are currently being written, although none has appeared as of this writing. A number of magazine articles were written when the Haldeman-Julius enterprises were at their peak. See "The Great Debunker—E. Haldeman-Julius" (516) by Gordon Stein in *Progressive World* and reference 414.

The Freethought Press Association was founded in New York in 1929 by Joseph Lewis, who was a great admirer of Paine and Ingersoll. As a result, he republished many of their works under his imprint. Lewis also wrote a number of books himself, most of which have been cited earlier. Lewis published his own books and magazines.

Some observations on a few of the more minor twentieth-century freethought publishers will complete our survey of American freethought publishing. A few books and pamphlets were published by Raymer's Book Store in Seattle, under the imprint of their journal, *The Crucible* (387). Madalyn Murray O'Hair issued a few of her own writings from her American Atheist Press. Arno Press of New York (although not a freethought publisher), republished a rather poorly chosen group of freethought books (British and American) in 1971-1972, which they called their Atheist Viewpoint series. Gordon Press of New York began to republish some classic freethought books, notably the works of Baron D'Holbach in English. Independent Publications of Paterson, New Jersey, has published a series of pamphlets, some reprints and some originals, including the works of Paine, Ingersoll, McCabe, and Fielding. The Truth Seeker Company continued publishing books and pamphlets in New York until the mid 1950s. Since its move to San Diego, it has reprinted a number of its earlier publications, along with reprints of other freethought classics. The Twin City Secularists published many freethought leaflets and flyers, while *The American Rationalist* (356) magazine reprinted articles that appeared in that journal. The Czech Rationalist Federation and the German Freie Gemeinden also published a number of books and pamphlets. (These are discussed more fully in Appendix I.) Frank Robinson's "Psychiana" at Moscow, Idaho, reprinted a few freethought books, including at least one of which Robinson claimed authorship by virtue of the fact that he had paraphrased the whole book (Kersey Graves' *The World's Sixteen Crucified Saviors* [302], which Robinson retitled *Crucified Gods Galore* [496]). The Friendship Liberal League of Philadelphia, publisher of *The Liberal* (453), also issued a few pamphlets over the years.

* * *

One of the United States' unique contributions to government is the principle of separation of church and state as enunciated in the First Amendment to the Constitution. The struggle to maintain this principle has occupied freethinkers (and others) throughout our entire history. From the McCollum v. Board of Education case in 1948 down to the present, the Supreme Court has reaffirmed and strengthened this principle. The definitive work in the field of American church and state relationships is the three-volume *Church and State in the United States* (519) by Anson Phelps Stokes. This work was later revised and abridged into a one-volume edition in 1964, with the same title (520). Either or both of these are the indispensable book(s) on church-state relations. A bibliography in the area of religion and public education was prepared by Lawrence Little, under the title *Religion and Public Education: A Bibliography* (455).

Many books have been written on some aspect of church-state relations. Among them are those in the following references: 353, 355, 363, 374, 378, 394, 407, 413, 428, 435, 436, 437, 439, 440, 456, 459, 470, 472, 476, 480, 481, 495, 513, 522, 523, 524, 527, 528, and 533.

An organization by the name of Americans United for the Separation of Church and State (usually just called Americans United) was organized in 1948 with headquarters in Silver Spring, Maryland. Since 1948, Americans United has published a monthly magazine named *Church and State* (382). It has a membership of 200,000.

* * *

The Unitarian church continued its steady but modest growth during the twentieth century. In 1961, the Unitarian and Universalist churches merged, for with the passing of time, their creeds had become very similar. Their official organs, *The Unitarian Register* and *The Universalist Leader,* were merged into the single *Unitarian Register and the Universalist Leader* (534). Today, the combined membership is about 210,000, with about 1,000 churches in the United States.

The Ethical Culture societies have continued to expand during the twentieth century. By 1975, a total of twenty-four societies had been established in many of the principal cities of the country. The membership increased from 2,400 in 1906 to about 5,000 today.

A new point of view called Humanism, sometimes termed Secular Humanism, also developed in this century. Humanism represents itself as a faith, a commitment, and a way of life. It is a religion without a God, a supernatural, or a sacred scripture. Its emphasis is on man, not God; on the here and now, not some hereafter; on man's salvation lying within himself, not in some external force. Some of the early advocates of the Humanist point of view were Charles Francis Potter, John Hassler Dietrich, and Curtis W. Reese. Some of these men were active in the cause of Humanism as early as the 1920s.

Charles Francis Potter (1885-1962), one of the pioneers in the development of Humanism, first became a minister in the Baptist church. His increasingly liberal point of view compelled him to leave the Baptist church and to join the Unitarian church, which he also found too conservative. He resigned from the Unitarian church in 1929 and established the First Humanist Society of New York. He devoted the remainder of his life to furthering Humanism. Potter wrote a number of books on Humanism and religious history, including those in references 482, 483, 484, 485, and 487. He also wrote an autobiography, *The Preacher and I* (486), which is also an excellent source of information on the history of Humanism.

John Hassler Dietrich (1878-1957) was trained as a minister in the Reformed church, but resigned to become a Unitarian minister. He served in Spokane, Washington, from 1911 to 1925, and in 1925, he went to Minneapolis, where he served the First Unitarian Church until 1938. While a Unitarian, he constantly preached on the Humanist point of view. From 1926 to 1933, the First Unitarian Society of Minneapolis published many of his sermons in a seven-volume set called *The Humanist Pulpit* (395). A biography of Dietrich entitled *The Circle of Earth* (396) was written by Margaret Winston Dietrich (as Carleton Winston). There is a biographical sketch of Dietrich in the *National Cyclopedia of American Biography* (473).

Curtis W. Reese, a Unitarian minister and former Dean of the Lincoln Centre in Chicago, precipitated the discussions that led to religious Humanism, by a challenging sermon at Des Moines, Iowa, in 1917 and an address at the Harvard Divinity School in 1920. These discussions by philosophers, teachers, writers, and clergyman resulted in the emergence of Humanism in religion, eventually culminating in the *Humanist Manifesto* in 1933. Reese wrote *Humanist Religion* (492).

William Floyd (1871-1944) also did much to further the cause of Humanism. Educated at Princeton, he became an editor and wrote a number of books about Humanism, including those listed in the following references: 400, 401, 402, 403. Floyd was also the editor of *The Arbitrator* (357). A biographical sketch appears in *Who's Who Among North American Authors* (441).

In 1933, the fifteen-point Humanist Manifesto was signed by thirty-four intellectuals: J. A. C. Fagginer Auer, E. Burdette Backus, Harry Elmer Barnes, L. M. Birkhead, Raymond B. Bragg, Edwin Arthur Burtt, Ernest Caldecott, A. J. Carlson, John Dewey, Albert C. Dieffenbach, John H. Dietrich, Bernard Fantus, William Floyd, F. H. Hankins, A. Eustace Haydon, Llewellyn Jones, Robert Morss Lovett, Harold P.

Marley, R. Lester Mondale, Charles Francis Potter, John Herman Randall, Jr., Curtis W. Reese, Oliver L. Reiser, Roy Wood Sellars, Clinton Lee Scott, Maynard Shipley, W. Frank Swift, V. T. Thayer, Eldred C. Vanderlaan, Joseph Walker, Jacob J. Weinstein, Frank S. C. Wicks, David Rhys Williams, and Edwin H. Wilson. When issued, the signers claimed that it was not a creed, but only an effort to express their point of agreement at the moment. In 1973, the seventeen-point Humanist Manifesto II appeared. It was signed by hundreds of Humanists. Both of these manifestos are included in a book called *Humanist Manifestos I and II* (425).

In 1941, the American Humanist Association was founded to act as a central agency for Humanists. It publishes a magazine called *The Humanist* (424) and holds annual conventions. In 1952, representatives from Humanist groups in many countries met in Amsterdam and formed the International Humanist and Ethical Union. Since that time, its congresses have been held in London (1957), Oslo (1962), Paris (1966), Boston (1970), and again in Amsterdam (1974). Today the association has about thirty local units located in most large cities in the United States.

One of the best statements of Humanism appears in *Humanism as a Philosophy* (432) by Corliss Lamont (1902-   ). Lamont was educated at Harvard and Columbia Universities and has served as a professor of philosophy, most recently at Columbia. In addition to the above book, Lamont is the author of *The Illusion of Immortality* (433). There is an autobiographical pamphlet about him entitled *My First Sixty Years* (434).

One of the best books on the history of Humanism is *Humanism as the Next Step* (471) by Lloyd and Mary Morain. The American Humanist Association's magazine, *The Humanist* (424), has been published since 1941 and is now issued six times a year. Beginning in 1969 until December 1977, *The Humanist* was published jointly by the American Ethical Union and the American Humanist Association. It is currently being published solely by the American Humanist Association. In 1976, it had a circulation of about 32,000.

BIBLIOGRAPHY

351. *Age of Reason, The,* a freethought periodical edited and published by Joseph Lewis in New York, 1937-1968. It was called

The Bulletin of the Freethinkers of America from 1937 to December 1943; *The Freethinker* from January 1944 to August 1949; *Common Sense* from September 1949 to October 1951; and *The Age of Reason* from November 1951 to December 1968.

352. Allen, Leslie H., ed. *Bryan and Darrow at Dayton.* New York: Arthur Lee & Co., 1925.

353. American Association of School Administrators. *Religion in the Public Schools: A Report of the Commission on Religion in the Public Schools.* Washington, D.C.: American Association of School Administrators, 1964.

354. *American Atheist, The,* a monthly freethought periodical published in Austin, Texas, and edited by Madalyn Murray O'Hair, 1964-present. It was the successor to *The Free Humanist* (405) of Philadelphia and was first published at Baltimore in 1964. Since then, it has been published in Honolulu and Austin.

355. American Civil Liberties Union. *Religious Liberty in the United States: A Survey of the Restraints on Religious Freedom.* New York: American Civil Liberties Union, 1939.

356. *American Rationalist, The,* a freethought periodical published at St. Louis by the American Rationalist Association, 1956-present. It was published monthly from 1956 to 1966, but since then as a bimonthly. It was also published from Chicago for a short time.

357. *Arbitrator, The,* a freethought periodical published monthly in New York, 1918-1943, and edited by William Floyd.

358. Asbury, Herbert. *Up from Methodism.* New York: Alfred A. Knopf, 1926.

359. *Atheist, The,* an atheist periodical published irregularly by the Truth Seeker Company, New York, 1947-1953, and edited by Woolsey Teller. It was recently revived at San Diego by James Hervey Johnson.

360. *Atheist Magazines: A Sampling, 1927-70.* New York: Arno Press, 1972. Includes an Introduction by Madalyn Murray O'Hair that must be used with great caution, since it contains factual errors.

361. Barnes, Harry Elmer. *The Twilight of Christianity.* New York: Vanguard Press, 1929. One of the best statements of the Humanist point of view by a distinguished historian.

362. Bartley, Robert F. *The Star-Studded Hoax of Christianity With Its Allied Gods.* Detroit: Harol, 1969.

363. Bates, Ernest Sutherland. *This Land of Liberty.* New York: Harper & Brothers, 1930.

364. Bestic, Allan. *Praise the Lord and Pass the Contribution.* New York: Taplinger Publishing Co., 1971.

365. Blanshard, Paul. *American Freedom and Catholic Power.* Boston: Beacon Press, 1949.

366. Blanshard, Paul. *Communism, Democracy and Catholic Power.* Boston: Beacon Press, 1951.

367. Blanshard, Paul. *Freedom and Catholic Power in Spain and Portugal: An American Interpretation.* Boston: Beacon Press, 1962.

368. Blanshard, Paul. *God and Man in Washington.* Boston: Beacon Press, 1960.

369. Blanshard, Paul. *The Irish and Catholic Power.* Boston: Beacon Press, 1953.

370. Blanshard, Paul. *Personal and Controversial: An Autobiography.* Boston: Beacon Press, 1973.

371. Blanshard, Paul. *Religion and the Schools: The Great Controversy.* Boston: Beacon Press, 1963.

372. Blanshard, Paul. *Some of My Friends Are Christian.* LaSalle, Ill.: Open Court, 1973.

373. Bode, Carl. *Mencken.* Carbondale, Ill.: Southern Illinois University Press, 1969.

374. Boles, Donald E. *The Bible, Religion, and the Public Schools.* Ames, Iowa: Iowa State University Press, 1961.

375. Boone, Abbott. *Our Hypocritical New National Motto: In God We Trust—A Study of the Congressional Substitution for E. Pluribus Unum and Its Theological Implications.* New York: Exposition Press, 1963.

376. Brooks, David M. *The Necessity of Atheism.* New York: Freethought Press Assoc., 1933.

377. Brudno, Ezra. *Ghosts of Yesterday.* New York: D. Appleton-Century Co., 1935.

378. Butts, R. Freeman. *The American Tradition in Religion and Education.* Boston: Beacon Press, 1950.

379. Calverton, V. F. *The Passing of the Gods.* New York: Charles Scribner's Sons, 1934.

380. Cardiff, Ira D. *What Great Men Think of Religion.* Boston: Christopher Publishing House, 1943. A collection of quotations, often poorly identified as to exact source.

381. Chesen, Eli S. *Religion May Be Hazardous to Your Health.* New York: Peter H. Wyden, 1972.

382. *Church and State,* a monthly magazine published at Silver Spring, Maryland, by Americans United for the Separation of Church

and State. It was published at Washington, D.C., from 1948 to November 1969, after which time it moved to Silver Spring. It is still being published.

383. Clampett, Frederick W. *Luther Burbank "Our Beloved Infidel":
His Religion of Humanity.* New York: Macmillan Co., 1926.

384. *Common Herd,* a quarterly freethought periodical published at Dallas, Texas, by Richard Potts, 1909-1940.

385. Croy, Homer. "Atheism Beckons to Our Youth." *World's Work* 54 (1927):18-26.

386. Croy, Homer. "Atheism Rampant in Our Schools." *World's Work* 54 (1927):140-147.

387. *Crucible, The,* a freethought periodical published at Seattle, Washington, 1916-1932. It was a weekly, 1916-1928, and a monthly 1929-1932.

388. *Crucible, The,* a freethought periodical published at Cass Lake, Duluth, and St. Paul, Minnesota, 1966-1972. It is now published irregularly from Mercedes, Texas.

389. Dark, Sidney, and Essex, R. S. *The War Against God.* New York: Abingdon Press, 1937.

390. Darrow, Clarence. *The Story of My Life.* New York: Charles Scribner's Sons, 1932.

391. De Camp, L. Sprague. *The Great Monkey Trial.* Garden City, N.Y.: Doubleday, 1968.

392. DeFord, Miriam A. *Up-Hill All the Way.* Yellow Springs, Ohio: Antioch Press, 1956. A biography of Maynard Shipley.

393. Demlinger, Floyd O. *Free Minds Venturing: An Essay on Realities and the Supernatural.* New York: Exposition Press, 1969.

394. Dierenfield, Richard B. *Religion in American Public Schools.* Washington, D.C.: Public Affairs Press, 1962.

395. Dietrich, John H. *The Humanist Pulpit.* Minneapolis: Unitarian Society of Minneapolis, 1926-1933, 7 vols. Contains the collected sermons of John H. Dietrich while he served as pastor at the Minneapolis Unitarian Church.

396. Dietrich, Margaret Winston (as Carleton Winston). *The Circle of Earth.* New York: G. P. Putnam's Sons, 1942.

397. Edward, Marshall. "Thomas A. Edison on Immortality." *The Columbian Magazine* 3 (1911):603-612.

398. Fielding, William J. *All the Lives I Have Lived.* Philadelphia: Dorrance & Co., 1972.

399. Fielding, William J. *The Shackles of the Supernatural.* Girard, Kans.: Haldeman-Julius Publications, 1938. Republished as a hard-

back book in New York by Vantage Press, 1969.

400. Floyd, William. *Christianity Cross-Examined.* New York: Arbitrator Press, 1941.

401. Floyd, William. *Humanizing Biblical Religion.* New York: Arbitrator Press, 1943.

402. Floyd, William. *The Mistakes of Jesus.* New York: Arbitrator Press, 1932.

403. Floyd, William. *Our Gods on Trial.* New York: Arbitrator Press, 1931.

404. Frank, Henry. *The Doom of Dogma and the Dawn of Truth.* New York: G. P. Putnam's Sons, 1901.

405. *Free Humanist, The,* a freethought periodical published at Philadelphia and edited by Ludwig Alt, 1959-1963. It was called *The Freethinker* during 1959 and part of 1960. In January 1964, it became *The American Atheist* (354), with Madalyn Murray (later O'Hair) as editor.

406. *Freethought Opinion,* a freethought periodical published at Paterson, New Jersey, six times a year, 1974-1975.

407. Frommer, Arthur, ed. *The Bible and the Public Schools.* New York: Frommer/Pasmantier Publishing Co., 1963.

408. Garrison, James H. *Unorthodox Facts.* Memphis, Tenn.: Chickasaw Publishers, 1940.

409. Gauvin, Marshall. *Fundamentals of Freethought.* New York: Peter Eckler Publishing Co., 1923.

410. Ginger, Ray. *Six Days or Forever? Tennessee v. John Thomas Scopes.* Boston: Beacon Press, 1958.

411. Grebstein, Sheldon Norman, ed. *Monkey Trial: The State of Tennessee vs. John Thomas Scopes.* Boston: Houghton Mifflin Co., 1960.

412. Grebstein, Sheldon Norman. *Sinclair Lewis.* New York: Twayne Publishers, 1962.

413. Griffith, William E. *Religion, the Courts and the Public Schools.* Cincinnati: W. H. Anderson Co., 1966.

414. Haldeman-Julius, Emanuel. *The First Hundred Million.* New York: Simon & Schuster, 1928.

415. Harris, Ben. *Human Gods.* Philadelphia: Dorrance & Co., 1939.

416. Harrison, Charles Yale. *Clarence Darrow.* New York: Jonathan Cape & Harrison Smith, 1931.

417. Herzog, Arthur. *The Church Trap.* New York: Macmillan Co., 1968.

418. Howard, Jane. "The Most Hated Woman in America." *Life* 56 (1964):91-94.

419. Howland, Arthur H. *Joseph Lewis:Enemy of God*. Boston: Stratford Co., 1932.

420. Howlett, Duncan. *The Fourth American Faith*. New York: Harper & Row, 1964.

421. Hubbard, Elbert II. *The Philosophy of Elbert Hubbard*. New York: William H. Wise & Co., 1930.

422. Hudson, Jay William. *The Old Faiths Perish*. New York: Appleton-Century Co., 1939.

423. Hughes, Rupert. *Why I Quit Going to Church*. New York: Freethought Press Association, 1934.

424. *Humanist, The,* a Humanist periodical, originally published monthly, but now as a bimonthly from Buffalo, New York. It began publication in 1941 and has been published from several cities (e.g., Yellow Springs, Ohio, San Francisco, and Buffalo). The first publication of the Humanist movement in the United States (i.e., the American Humanist Association) was *The New Humanist* (Chicago, 1928-1936). This was later revived under the title *The Humanist Bulletin* (Chicago, 1938-1941) and then renamed *The Humanist* in 1941.

425. *Humanist Manifestos I and II,* Buffalo: Prometheus Books, 1973.

426. *Humanitarian Review,* a rationalist and Ethical Culture magazine published monthly at Los Angeles, 1903-1911. It was edited by Singleton W. Davis and merged into *The Ingersoll Memorial Beacon* (427) in December 1911.

427. *Ingersoll Memorial Beacon, The,* a monthly freethought periodical that tried to continue the expression of Robert G. Ingersoll's views. It was published at Chicago, 1904-1913. The name was changed to *Freethought Beacon* in 1912.

428. Johnson, Alvin, and Yost, Frank H. *Separation of Church and State in the United States*. Minneapolis: University of Minnesota Press, 1948.

429. Johnson, James Hervey. *Superior Men: A Book of Reason for the Man of Vision*. San Diego: James Hervey Johnson, 1949.

430. Josephson, Matthew. *Edison: A Biography*. New York: McGraw-Hill, 1959.

431. Kemler, Edgar. *The Irreverent Mr. Mencken*. Boston: Little Brown & Co., 1950.

432. Lamont, Corliss. *Humanism as a Philosophy*. New York: Philosophical Library, 1949. In later editions, the title was changed to *The Philosophy of Humanism* and the publisher to Frederick Ungar Publishing Co., 1957.

433. Lamont, Corliss, *The Illusion of Immortality*. New York: G. P. Putnam's Sons, 1935.

434. Lamont, Corliss. *My First Sixty Years.* New York: Basic Pamphlets, 1962.

435. Larson, Martin A. *Church Wealth and Business Income.* New York: Philosophical Library, 1965.

436. Larson, Martin A. *The Churches: Their Riches, Revenues and Immunities.* Washington, D.C.: Robert B. Luce, 1969.

437. Larson, Martin A. *Praise the Lord for Tax Exemption: How the Churches Grow Rich While the Cities and You Grow Poor.* Washington, D.C.: Robert B. Luce, 1969.

438. Larson, Martin A. *The Religion of the Occident.* New York: Philosophical Library, 1959. A revised edition was published in 1977 by New Republic Books (Washington, D.C.) with the new title *The Story of Christian Origins.*

439. Larson, Martin A. *When Parochial Schools Close: A Study in Educational Financing.* Washington, D.C.: Robert B. Luce, 1972.

440. Laubach, John Herbert. *School Prayers, Congress, the Courts, and the Public.* Washington, D.C.: Public Affairs Press, 1969.

441. Lawrence, Alberta, ed. *Who's Who Among North American Authors.* Los Angeles: Golden Syndicate Publishing Co., 1939.

442. Lawrence, Jerome, and Lee, Robert E. *Inherit the Wind.* New York: Random House, 1955.

443. Leuba, James H. *The Belief in God and Immortality.* Boston: Sherman, French & Co., 1916. Leuba (1868-1946) was a distinguished psychologist. After an exhaustive study, he concluded that the more distinguished scientists had less belief in God and immortality than the less distinguished scientists. See no. 446 below.

444. Leuba, James H. *God or Man?* New York: Henry Holt, 1933.

445. Leuba, James H. *The Reformation of the Churches.* Boston: Beacon Press, 1950.

446. Leuba, James H. "Religious Beliefs of American Scientists" *Harper's Magazine* 169 (1934):291-300. This article was a followup to the study described in no. 443 above.

447. Lewis, Joseph. *Atheism and Other Addresses.* New York: Freethought Press Association, 1941.

448. Lewis, Joseph. *An Atheist Manifesto.* New York: Freethought Press Association, 1954.

449. Lewis, Joseph. *The Bible Unmasked.* New York: Freethought Press Association, 1926.

450. Lewis, Joseph. *The Ten Commandments.* New York: Freethought Press Association, 1946.

451. Lewis, Joseph. *The Tyranny of God.* New York: Freethought Press Association, 1921.

452. Lewis, Sinclair. *Elmer Gantry.* New York; Harcourt, Brace, 1927.

453. *Liberal, The,* a monthly freethought periodical published in Philadelphia by the Friendship Liberal League, 1947-circa1970.

454. Liston, Robert. "Mrs. Murray's War on God." *Saturday Evening Post* 237 (July 11, 1964):83-87.

455. Little, Lawrence. *Religion and Public Education: A Bibliography.* Pittsburgh: University of Pittsburgh Book Center, 1968.

456. Lowell, C. Stanley. *The Great Church-State Fraud.* Washington, D.C.: Robert B. Luce, 1973.

457. McCabe, Joseph. *Crime and Religion.* Clifton, N.J.: Progressive World, 1954.

458. McCarthy, William. *The Bible, Church and God.* New York: Truth Seeker Co., 1946.

459. McCollum, Vashti Cromwell. *One Woman's Fight.* New York: Doubleday, 1950.

460. [Macdonald, George E.]. *A Short History of the Inquisition.* New York: Truth Seeker Co., 1907.

461. McLoughlin, Emmett. *American Culture and Catholic Schools.* New York: Lyle Stuart, 1960.

462. McLoughlin, Emmett. *Crime and Immorality in the Catholic Church.* New York: Lyle Stuart, 1962.

463. McLoughlin, Emmett. *An Inquiry into the Assassination of Abraham Lincoln.* New York: Lyle Stuart, 1963.

464. McLoughlin, Emmett. *People's Padre: An Autobiography.* Boston: Beacon Press, 1954.

465. Manchester, William. *Disturber of the Peace: The Life of H. L. Mencken.* New York: Harper & Brothers, 1950.

466. Matson, Wallace I. *The Existence of God.* Ithaca, N.Y.: Cornell University Press, 1965.

467. Maylone, W. Edgar. *Thrown at the Atheist's Head.* Philadelphia: Dorrance & Co., 1973.

468. Mencken, Henry L. *A Treatise on the Gods.* New York: Alfred A. Knopf, 1930.

469. *Militant Atheist, The,* a monthly freethought periodical (in newspaper format) published by E. Haldeman-Julius at Girard, Kansas, 1933. It was edited by Joseph McCabe and lasted only nine issues (January through September 1933). Other periodicals published by E. Haldeman-Julius were *The Haldeman-Julius Weekly,* 1922-1926, after which time it changed its name to *The American Freeman,* 1929-1951; *The Haldeman-Julius Monthly,* 1924-1928, at which time it changed its name to *The Debunker,* 1928-1932; *The Haldeman-Julius*

Quarterly, 1926-1929; *The Joseph McCabe Magazine,* 1930-1931; and *The Critic and Guide,* 1947-1951.

470. Moehlman, Conrad Henry. *The Wall of Separation Between Church and State.* Boston: Beacon Press, 1951.

471. Morain, Lloyd, and Morain, Mary. *Humanism As the Next Step.* Boston: Beacon Press, 1954.

472. Morgan, Richard E. *The Supreme Court and Religion.* New York: Free Press, 1972.

473. *National Cyclopedia of American Biography.* New York: James T. White & Co., 1893-present (annual publication).

474. Noble, Iris. *Clarence Darrow Defense Attorney.* New York: Julian Messner, 1958.

475. O'Connor, Richard. *Sinclair Lewis.* New York: McGraw-Hill, 1971.

476. O'Hair, Madalyn Murray. *An Atheist Epic: Bill Murray, The Bible and the Baltimore Board of Education.* Austin, Tex.: American Atheist Press, 1970.

477. O'Hair, Madalyn Murray. *Freedom Under Siege: The Impact of Organized Religion on Your Liberty and Your Pocketbook.* Los Angeles: J. P. Tarcher, 1974.

478. O'Hair, Madalyn Murray. *What on Earth Is an Atheist!* Austin, Tex.: American Atheist Press, 1969.

479. *Open Mind, The,* a monthly freethought periodical published at Newark, New Jersey. It began publication in 1960 and was discontinued a few years later.

480. Pfeffer, Leo. *Church, State and Freedom.* Boston: Beacon Press, 1953.

481. Pfeffer, Leo. *God, Caesar and the Constitution.* Boston: Beacon Press, 1974. One of the best and most comprehensive books on church-state relations. It ably combines encyclopedic breadth and depth with conciseness and readability.

482. Potter, Charles F. *The Faith Men Live By.* New York: Prentice-Hall, 1954.

483. Potter, Charles F. *Humanism: A New Religion.* New York: Simon & Schuster, 1930.

484. Potter, Charles F. *Humanizing Religion.* New York: Harper & Brothers, 1933.

485. Potter, Charles F. *Is That in the Bible?* Garden City, N.Y.: Garden City Publishing Co., 1933.

486. Potter, Charles F. *The Preacher and I.* New York: Crown Publishers, 1951. The autobiography of Potter.

487. Potter, Charles F. *The Story of Religion.* New York: Simon & Schuster, 1929.

488. *Progressive Forum,* a monthly freethought periodical edited and published at Los Angeles by Charles Calhoun, 1923-1930.

489. *Progressive World,* a freethought periodical published by the United Secularists of America. It began as a monthly at Clifton, New Jersey, in 1947, but changed to a bimonthly in April 1974. It moved from Clifton in 1959 and was then published in Los Angeles until 1970, at which time it moved to the San Francisco area. It is still published.

490. *Queen Silver's Magazine,* a quarterly freethought periodical published at Inglewood and then Hawthorne, California (the location remained the same, but post office boundaries changed) by Queen Silver, 1923-1928.

491. *Rationalist, The,* a monthly Humanist periodical published by the Independent Religious Society of Chicago and edited by M. M. Mangasarian, 1912-1916. It contained a printed version of Mangasarian's weekly lectures.

492. Reese, Curtis. *Humanist Religion.* New York: Macmillan Co., 1931.

493. Riddle, Oscar. *The Unleashing of Evolutionary Thought.* New York: Vantage Press, 1954.

494. *Ripsaw, The,* a freethought periodical published at South Bend, Indiana, and edited by Virgil McClain. It began publication in 1955 and merged with *The Free Humanist* (405) in 1963.

495. Robertson, D. B. *Should Churches Be Taxed?* Philadelphia: Westminster Press, 1968.

496. Robinson, Frank B. *Crucified Gods Galore.* Moscow, Idaho: Psychiana, 1933. A rewrite of *The World's Sixteen Crucified Saviors* (302) by Kersey Graves.

497. Robinson, James Harvey. *The Human Comedy: As Devised and Directed by Mankind Itself.* New York: Harper & Brothers, 1937.

498. Rocca, Bernard T., Sr. *Faith, Fact and Reason,* vol. 1. [Manila]: Bernard T. Rocca, 1964.

499. Rocca, Bernard T., Sr. *Faith, Fact and Reason,* vol. 2. New York: Carleton Press, 1973.

500. Rocca, Bernard T., Sr. *Fitting in the Pieces.* [Manila]: Bernard T. Rocca, 1964.

501. Runyon, G. Vincent. *Why I Left the Ministry and Became an Atheist.* San Diego: Superior Books, 1959.

502. Russell, Bertrand. *Why I Am Not a Christian and Other Es-*

says on Religion and Related Subjects. New York: Simon & Schuster, 1957. Although Russell was not an American, this book achieved wide distribution and readership in the United States.

503. Schneider, Herbert W. *Religion in Twentieth Century America.* Cambridge, Mass.: Harvard University Press, 1952.

504. Schorer, Mark. *Sinclair Lewis: An American Life.* New York: McGraw-Hill, 1961.

505. Schuster, M. Lincoln, ed. *A Treasury of the World's Greatest Letters.* New York: Simon & Schuster, 1940.

506. Scopes, John T. *Center of the Storm: Memoirs of John T. Scopes.* New York: Holt, Rinehart & Winston, 1966.

507. Scott, Richard. *A Game of Chess: A Study in Atheism.* New York: Philosophical Library, 1954.

508. Scriven, Michael. *Primary Philosophy.* New York: McGraw-Hill, 1966.

509. Settle, Mary L. *The Scopes Trial.* New York: Franklin Watts, 1972.

510. Shipley, Maynard. *The War on Modern Science.* New York: Alfred A. Knopf, 1927.

511. Sinclair, Upton. *The Profits of Religion.* Pasadena, Calif.: Upton Sinclair, 1918.

512. Smith, Charles. *Sensism: The Philosophy of the West.* New York: Truth Seeker Co., 1956, 2 vols.

513. Smith, Elwyn A. *Religious Liberty in the United States: The Development of Church-State Thought Since the Revolutionary Era.* Philadelphia: Fortress Press, 1972.

514. Smith, George H. *Atheism: The Case Against God.* Los Angeles: Nash Publishing Co., 1974. Probably the best work on the subject of the arguments for the existence of God.

515. Smith, Homer. *Man and His Gods.* Boston: Little, Brown & Co., 1952.

516. Stein, Gordon. "The Great Debunker—E. Haldeman-Julius." *Progressive World* 14 (1971):13-20.

517. Steiner, Franklin. *Religion and Roguery.* New York: Truth Seeker Co., 1924.

518. Stenerson, Douglas C. *H. L. Mencken: Iconoclast from Baltimore.* Chicago: University of Chicago Press, 1975.

519. Stokes, Anson Phelps. *Church and State in the United States.* New York: Harper & Brothers, 1950, 3 vols. The definitive work on church-state relations.

520. Stokes, Anson Phelps, and Pfeffer, Leo. *Church and State*

in the United States. New York: Harper & Row, 1964. A one-volume revised edition and abridgement of no. 519 above.

521. Stone, Irving. *Clarence Darrow for the Defense.* New York: Doubleday, Doran & Co., 1941.

522. Swancara, Frank. *Obstruction of Justice by Religion.* Denver: W. H. Courtright, 1936.

523. Swancara, Frank. *Religion and Crime: The Anti-Social and Debilitant Influence of Religious Emotions and Concepts.* Girard, Kans.: Haldeman-Julius Publications, 1947.

524. Swancara, Frank. *Separation of Religion and Government.* New York: Truth Seeker Co., 1950.

525. Teller, Woolsey. *The Atheism of Astronomy.* New York: Truth Seeker Co., 1938.

526. Teller, Woolsey. *Essays of an Atheist.* New York: Truth Seeker Co., 1945.

527. Thayer, V. T. *The Attack upon the American Secular School.* Boston: Beacon Press, 1951.

528. Thayer, V. T. *Religion in Public Education.* New York: Viking Press, 1947.

529. Tichenor, Henry M. *The Life and Exploits of Jehovah.* St. Louis: Phil Wagner, 1915.

530. Tichenor, Henry M. *The Sorceries and Scandals of Satan.* St. Louis: Phil Wagner, 1917.

531. Tichenor, Henry M. *Tales of Theology.* St. Louis: Melting Pot Publishing Co., 1918.

532. Tompkins, Jerry R., ed. *D-Day at Dayton: Reflections of the Scopes Trial.* Baton Rouge, La.: Louisiana State University Press, 1965.

533. Tussman, Joseph, ed. *The Supreme Court on Church and State.* New York: Oxford University Press, 1962.

534. *Unitarian Register and the Universalist Leader,* a weekly organ of the Unitarian-Universalist churches. It resulted from the merging of *The Unitarian Register* and *The Universalist Leader* in 1961. *The Unitarian Register* had been published under various names since 1821; *The Universalist Leader* had also been published under various names since 1819.

535. Van Doren, Carl. *Sinclair Lewis.* New York: Doubleday, Doran & Co., 1933.

536. Vetter, George B., and Green, Martin. "Personality and Group Factors in the Making of Atheists." *Journal of Abnormal and Social Psychology* 17 (1932):179-194.

537. Washburn, Lemuel K. *Is the Bible Worth Reading and Other Essays.* New York: Truth Seeker Co., 1911.

538. Weinberg, Arthur, ed. *Attorney for the Damned.* New York: Simon & Schuster, 1967. A biography of Clarence Darrow.

539. Wheless, Joseph. *Forgery in Christianity: A Documented Record of the Foundations of the Christian Religion.* New York: Alfred A. Knopf, 1930.

540. Wheless, Joseph. *Is It God's Word?* New York: Alfred A. Knopf, 1926.

541. *Who's Who in America.* Chicago: Marquis Who's Who, Inc., 1899/1900-present. An annual volume.

542. Williams, Hayward A. *Fifty Years to Atheism.* New York: Vantage Press, 1966.

APPENDIX I

★ ★ ★ ★ ★ ★ ★ ★ ★

Notes on Ethnic Freethought

Generally, America's immigrants tended to settle in areas already inhabited by their countrymen or in places close to them. This practice tended to perpetuate the use of the immigrants' particular native language and helped preserve the immigrant groups' customs and religious beliefs.

While many ethnic groups formed freethought groups, the organizations were for the most part local and not national. Two exceptions were the German Free Religious Congregations (Freie Gemeinden) and the Czech Rationalist Groups, often called the Bohemian Rationalists. Both were large enough to allow them to organize in several states and to have their own schools and freethought publications.

Only fragmentary information is available on some of the other ethnic freethought groups. We have gathered together whatever data we could in order to at least open the door to research in this area. Almost nothing seems to have been written on these groups in English. We hope that others can add to the partial information we have discovered.

The Freie Gemeinden or Free Congregations originated in both the Protestant and Catholic churches in Germany between 1840 and 1846 as a protest against the strict orthodoxy of those churches. Those who joined the Freie Gemeinden in Germany insisted that an individual had the right to hold those religious beliefs which his own reading and study led him to accept as reasonable and consistent with his knowledge of the world. Every attempt was made to avoid the establishment of a hierarchy within the Freie Gemeinden, for such a structure would be too much of a reminder of the churches from which they were trying to escape. A "speaker" was substituted for a clergyman, and decisions were made by democratic vote among the members.

The first Freie Gemeinden in America were founded in 1850, following the exodus of many dissident Germans from Germany. Before that time, however, America already had a number of German freethought newspapers which were unrelated to the Freie Gemeinden. In 1834, *Alte und Neue Welt* was founded in Philadelphia, with Samuel Ludvigh as the editor. *Der Freisinnige* was established in Philadelphia in 1838 and *Freie Presse* in 1848. In New York, *Vernunftgläubiger* was established in 1838 but died shortly thereafter. In 1840, Cincinnati saw the birth of *Lichtfreund,* which was later moved to Hermann, Missouri; it was succeeded by *Hermanner Wochenblatt.* Other Cincinnati papers were the *Antipfaff* (founded in 1842) and *Der Hochwachter* (1845-1846). In St. Louis, another *Der Freisinnige* appeared in 1846. Perhaps the most famous of these early German freethought papers was another Samuel Ludvigh creation, *Die Fackel* which originated in New York (1843-1847) and was revived in Baltimore (1849-1850).

In North America, the immigrant members of the Freie Gemeinden formed a national organization known as the Bund der freie Gemeinden von Nordamerika. This loose federation of local societies published an annual report called *Bericht des Vorstandes des Freidenker-bundes von Nordamerika* (Milwaukee) and held annual meetings or conventions.

Two important leaders of the Freie Gemeinden in Germany, Eduard Schroeter and Friedrich Schuenemann-Pott, clashed with the religious authorities and emigrated to the United States in the 1850s with prison records and/or deportation orders accompanying them. Schroeter settled in Wisconsin, where he founded the journal *Der Humanist* in Milwaukee (1851-1853) and organized many Free Congregations in Wisconsin. For more information on Schroeter, see J. J. Schlicher's article, "Eduard Schroeter the Humanist," in the *Wisconsin Magazine of History* (Part I in December 1944 and Part II in March 1945).

Schuenemann-Pott became a "speaker" in Philadelphia and later in San Francisco where he published the magazine *Blätter für freies religioeses Leben* (1856-1877). The *Blätter* contains a series of reminiscences by Schroeter, which ran in the magazine from 1860 to 1867. Schuenemann-Pott's reminiscences were also published in the *Blätter* from November 1873 through May 1875.

An article describing some of the activities and personalities of the Freie Gemeinden is Berenice Cooper's "Die Freie Gemeinde—Freethinkers on the Frontier," which appeared in *Minesota History* 41 (1968):53-60. Schuenemann-Pott also wrote a short history of his organization, in German, under the title *Die Freie Gemeinde* (Philadelphia: B. G. Stephan, 1861). Of course, this work covers the history only up to the 1861 publication date. Another history of the American Freie Gemeinden is the *Geschichtliche Mittheilungen über die Deutschen Freie Gemeinden von Nordamerika,* written and published by the Deutschen Freie Gemeinden von Philadelphia in 1877. Again, because of the relatively early date of publication, this is not a complete history. Other short histories include Max Hempel's *Was Sind die Freie Gemeinden?* (St. Louis: Verlag des Bundes-Vororts, 1902).

There were other periodical publications of the German-speaking freethought movement in the United States. *Der Freigeist* was published in Boston from 1873 to 1875. *Blitzstrahlen* was a Milwaukee publication which seems to have had only one issue in 1875. The *Freidenker* was published in Milwaukee from 1872 to 1917. It then moved to New Ulm, Minnesota, as described below. The *Freidenker* was perhaps the major publication of the U.S. Freie Gemeinden. An annual *Freidenker-Almanach* was published in Milwaukee by the Dörflinger/Freidenker Publishing Company from 1878 to 1899. *Das Freie Wort* was a successor to the *Freidenker* and began publication in Milwaukee in 1932, lasting until 1971. *Lucifer* (called *Arminia* after 1896) was published in Milwaukee from 1881 to 1898. *Der Pfaffenspiegel* came out in Chicago from 1906 to 1911. It was largely anti-clerical in content. Another paper called *Der Freidenker* (not to be confused with its Milwaukee cousin of the same name and year of founding) was published briefly in New York, beginning in 1872. *Der Arme Teufel* was published in Detroit from 1884 to 1898.

Several freethought *newspapers* were published in German after the founding of the Freie Gemeinden in 1850. Among them were *Hahnenruf* (New York City, 1851- ?) and *Morgenröthe* (Buffalo, N.Y., 1853?). There were also the *Volksfreund* (1847-1855) and *Banner* (1850-1855, which absorbed the *Volksfreund* (and in 1855 changed its name to the *Banner and Volksfreund,* 1855-1880). Both of these papers were published in Milwaukee. In Boston, a small Free Congregation published a newspaper called *Neu-England Zeitung* for a short time, beginning in 1852. There were also the weekly *Wilde Rosen* (Philadelphia, date unknown), the *Beobachter am Ohio* (Louisville, Ky., 1845-1853?), *Menschenrechte* (Cincinnati, 1853), *Freie Blätter* (Albany, N.Y., 1852-1896?), the *Freie Presse von Indiana* (Indianapolis, 1853-1866), and the Cleveland *Wächter am Erie* (1852-1893, at which time it merged with the *Anzeiger,* which had been published from 1866 to 1893, to form the *Wächter und Anzeiger,* which was published until 1900).

Often closely allied with the Freie Gemeinden in the period before 1870 were the socialist German organizations known as the Turnverein (the Turners). In this early period, many members of the Turnverein were in religious agreement with the Free Congregations, but the Turners were not so much a religious organization as an athletic association, with political leanings. Therefore, many of their publications are not described here. It should be noted, however, that the publication of the Milwaukee *Freidenker* was taken over by the Turner Publishing Company at New Ulm, Minnesota, in 1917. This publication continued until about 1932. The Turners had their own magazine called *Americanische Turnzeitung,* which was published at Milwaukee from 1885 until 1933.

Although there were signs of cooperation between the Turners and the Free Congregations in the pre-1870 period, the two groups had distinct ideological differences. The reunification of Germany by Bismarck in 1870 removed the major reason for the Turners' existence. After that time, they became much more conservative. In fact, the publication of the *Freidenker* by the Turner Publishing Company in 1917 should be viewed as strictly a business proposition, and not as an ideological venture.

Today the Freie Gemeinden movement is virtually dead. Some of the buildings they used are still standing (e.g., in Milwaukee and Sauk City, Wisconsin), but there are no longer any active congregations, publishing companies, or meetings. Many of the former members have now joined the English-speaking freethought groups.

The Czechs had the largest ethnic freethought movement in America, both in terms of total membership and amount of property owned. The movement had a number of schools of its own, in addition to club buildings and publications. The Czech rationalist movement was founded in about 1850 in New York City by Vojta Naprstek. He eventually settled in Milwaukee, where he published a liberal weekly, the *Flug Blatter.* The *Pokrok* first appeared in Chicago in 1867; moved to Racine, Wisconsin, for a short time in 1868; and ended up in Cleveland during 1875-1878. The first editor was Joseph Pastor; F. B. Zdrůbek (known as "the archpropagandist of atheism") later became editor. *Pokrok* was anti-clerical and very outspoken during its eleven-year existence (1867-1878).

In 1870, the Congregation of Bohemian Free Thinkers (Svobodná Obec) was established in Chicago. Its first publication was the newspaper *Svornost,* which began in Chicago in 1875 under the editorship of F. B. Zdrůbek. In 1877, *Duch Času* began publication in Chicago and lasted until just after World War II. It was a weekly, edited by August Geringer, one of the major Czech-American freethought publishers. *Svojan* began in Chicago in 1894 and was published there until 1924. At this time, *Svojan* merged with *Věk Rozumu,* a newspaper that had started in New York in 1910 and had moved to the Chicago area in the early 1920s. It is still being published at Berwyn, Illinois. There was another (unrelated) publication called *Svojan* in Chicago in 1873.

Around 1911, Frank Iška, the so-called Czech Ingersoll, began his work for freethought. Iška was the editor of a journal called *Vesmír,* which was published in Oklahoma City in 1909 and in Chicago from 1910 to 1921. The Czech Rationalist Federation had been founded in 1907, but was not considered the prime organization for Czech freethought in the United States until later. Another freethought publication, this one designed for the children in the Czech rationalist schools, was *Svobodná Škola.* This journal began in Oak Park, Illinois, in 1897 and is still published from Berwyn, Illinois. An early publication, originating in Cleveland, was *Dennice Novověku,* which existed from 1877 to about 1914. *Rovnosî Ļudu* was a Slovak newspaper with freethought leanings during its early years. It was published in Chicago from 1906 to 1926. It changed its name to *Denník Rovnosî Ļudu* in 1926 and finally to *Ļùdový Denník* in 1935. *Hlasatel* (later called *Denní Hlasatel*) was a Czech newspaper in Chicago, which was freethought in tendency during its first few years. It began in 1891 and is still published today.

So many small or minor Czech freethought magazines were published during the 1870-1910 period that a simple list, with comments where needed, will be given.

Osvěta Americká (Omaha, 1903-1916). Preceded some years previously (1898-1900) by *Osvěta,* also of Omaha; *Osvěta* preceded in Omaha by *Dělnické Listy* (1894-1898).

Dělnik Americký, a daily newspaper (New York, 1882-1886). Name changed to *New Yorské Listy* (1886-1966). Another *New Yorské Listy* published in New York (1874-1878); name changed to *Novoyorské Centennální Listy* in 1876.

Havlíček (Oklahoma City, 1908-circa 1910).

Orgán Bratrstva of the Czechoslovak Society of America (Oak Park, Illinois, 1891-1932). Name changed in 1932 to *Orgán Československých Spolkù v Americe* and finally to *Orgán C.S.A. (C.S.A. Journal).*

Nové Proudy (Cleveland, 1909).

Věstník Jednoty Táboritů (St. Louis, Chicago, 1910-1932).

Americký Legionář, (Chicago, 1919-1920).

Volná Myšlenka (Houston, Texas, 1919-1932).

Volné Směry (New York, 1903).

Pokrok Západu (Omaha, circa 1871).
Čechoslovan (Cleveland, 1909).
Českoamerické Kacířské Epištoly (Chicago, 1908-1909).
Žert A Pravda, a supplement to *Dennice Novověku* (Cleveland, 1898-1902).
Šotek, a satirical rationalist weekly (Chicago, 1893-1905).
Orgán Jednoty Svobodomyslných, another F. B. Zdrůbek publication (Cedar Rapids, Iowa, 1871).
Pravda (Cleveland, circa 1871).
Hlas Jednoty Svobodomyslných, a monthly (Iowa City, 1872-1873; Chicago, 1873; Milwaukee, 1876; New York, 1880-1881).
Amerikán (Chicago, 1875-1948), mostly reprinted articles from the newspaper *Svornost.*
Chicagský Věstník, a daily newspaper; Geringer the publisher (Chicago, 1873-1880).
Amerika, a Geringer publication (Chicago, 1888-1897).

The book publications of the Czech rationalist movement in the United States consisted largely of translations into Czech of English language freethought books. Among the authors translated were Paine, Volney, Mangasarian, and Ingersoll. Many important original publications were also published, among them commemorative volumes published to mark the centennial or other anniversary of the founding of various organizations. Some of these volumes are important as histories of those organizations. An example is the fiftieth anniversary of the founding of the Czech Rationalist Cemetery which prompted the publication of a 319-page volume entitled *Padesátileté Jubileum českého národního hřbitova v Chicagu Illinois.* The volume is full of pictures of Czech rationalists and is a virtual history of Czech rationalism in Chicago. Another example is *Památník sdružených svobodomyslných škol v Chicagu a okolí 1930,* which is a history of the Czech rationalist schools in Chicago.

Other original Czech rationalist books printed in America include Josef Král's *Víra a věda* (ten freethought essays), published in Chicago by Geringer; Král's biography, *John Hus* (Chicago, 1915); a history of Czech freethinking Americans called *Svobodomyslným Čechům americkým* (Chicago, 1914); and the *Constitution of the Czechoslovak Rationalist Federation of America* (Chicago, 1928), which was published in both Czech and English language versions.

In addition to August Geringer, publishers of Czech freethought pamphlets and books included Václav Šnajdr (Cleveland), Rosický (Omaha) and Bárta-Letovský (St. Louis). Often, such publishers also edited and published one of the Czech freethought periodicals.

Although the Czech-American rationalist movement today is not nearly as active as before, it is far from dead. Active meetings are still held in Cleveland, Houston, and Chicago by the Czech Rationalist Federation; five school groups continue to meet on Saturdays to teach children Czech culture and language; the federation still owns one school building (although it is not actively used as a school); and two publications are produced: *Věk Rozumu* and *Svobodná Škola* (both of which are discussed above).

While no other ethnic group had as large an organized freethought movement as did the Czechs and Germans, other nationalities did have some freethought activity. The Lithuanians, Poles, Swedes, Finns, Norwegians, Jews, and Italians, among others, published freethought literature, and several other groups had distinctly anti-clerical leanings as expressed through their publications.

The Lithuanian-Americans had several freethought publications: *Sake* (Chicago, 1913-1916) whose title was later changed to *Kardas* (Chicago, 1916-1923); another magazine called *Sake* (Chicago, 1926-1928; *Laisvamanis* (Chicago, circa 1938); *Ragna,* a monthly newspaper (Chicago, 1903 only); *Kurejas* (Chicago, 1900 only); *Dievo Rykste* (Chicago, 1912), an anti-clerical publication; *Darbininkas* (Chicago, 1903), a socialist, anti-clerical publication; and *Laisvoji Mintis* (Scranton, Pennsylvania, 1910-1914; Chicago, 1914-1915). A Lithuanian Freethinker's Alliance (Myl etojai Teisybes) existed in Chicago during 1900-1905.

Very little information about the Polish-American freethought movement is available, probably because it was not very large or organized into groups. They did have at least four freethought publications, however: *Dziennik Ludowy,* a freethought/socialist periodical (Chicago, 1907-1925); *Bicz Bozy* ("The Whip of God"), which existed in three different formats (see below); *Wolna Myśl* (Springfield, Massachusetts, 1923-1933); and another freethought periodical of the same name (Chicago, 1912-1915?). *Bicz Bozy* was the name given three different magazines: a satirical, anti-clerical magazine (Chicago, 1909-1918), a similar magazine (Chicago, 1927-1928), and a third (New York, 1934). *Mlotek Duchowny* (Utica, New York, 1910-1912) was an anti-clerical weekly.

There never was a Greek-American freethought movement as such in the United States, but one publication with a freethought outlook did exist. It was a weekly newspaper called *Loxias,* which was published in Chicago from 1908 to about 1921.

The Norwegian-Americans had a freethought organization that was closely associated with the socialists. Marcus Thrane, the most important figure in the Norwegian-American socialist/freethought movement, published a newspaper called *Norske Americane* in Chicago from 1866 to 1867. He then published a monthly magazine called *Dagslyset* in Chicago from 1869 to 1876 which moved to Becker, Minnesota, from 1876 to about 1878. Thrane also wrote a freethought book called *The Wisconsin Bible* and edited a newspaper in Chicago (1878-1884) named *Den Nye Tid.* The freethinkers' organization in the United States which had Norwegian and other Scandinavian members was called Den Skandinaviske Fritenkerforening. A man named Paoli was its leader for a time; no other information on Paoli is available.

The Serbians had a large number of socialist publications, many of which were distinctly anti-clerical, but they did not have a separate freethought movement as such. Some of their socialist publications were *Slobodna Misao* (Detroit, 1923-1926), *Volja,* an anarchist paper (New York, 1910-1914), *Radnik* (Chicago, 1917-1928), *Radnička Borba* (Cleveland, 1908-1966), *Narodni Glas* (Chicago, 1911), *Slobodna* (San Francisco, 1911-1914), *Slobodna Reč* (Pittsburgh, 1934-1946), *Slobodna Tribuna* (Seattle, 1910-1915 + 1931, and another of the same name in Tacoma, Washington, 1922-1928), *Sloga* (New York, circa 1906), and *Radnika Straža* (Chicago, 1907-1918).

The Slovenians had a freethought organization in Chicago called Zveza Slovenskih Svobdomiselv Ameriki, but the dates for this organization are not clear. They published a weekly newspaper called *Prosvieta* in Chicago in the early 1900s, and another called *Čas,* about the same time, which was anti-clerical. *Glas Svobode,* a weekly Chicago freethought newspaper (1901-1928?), also used its presses to publish freethought pamphlets in Slovenian. Evan Molik, an editor and author, expressed anti-clerical and rationalist views in many Slovenian periodicals.

The Finnish-American community had an important involvement with the socialists and socialist publications, but they cannot truly be called freethought, even though they were anti-clerical and against organized religion. Some of these publications, all of them newspapers, were *Sosialisti* (Duluth, Minnesota, 1915-1916), *Toveri* (Astoria, Oregon, 1921-1926) and its sister publication, *Toveritar* (Astoria, Oregon, 1915-1930), *Teollisuustyöläinen* (Duluth, 1916-1917), *Työmies* (Superior, Wisconsin, 1910-1950), and *Raivaaja* (Fitchburg, Massachusetts, 1905 to the present). Only one newspaper, *Aika,* could truly be called freethought; it was published in Sointula, British Columbia, Canada, from 1903 to 1904.

Several Finnish-American magazines had a freethought slant, although, again, most were primarily socialist in orientation. Among these were *Lapatossu* (Superior, Wisconsin, circa 1912-1920), *Säkenia* (Fitchburg, Massachusetts, circa 1910-1921), and *Nykyaika* (Fitchburg, 1922-1929).

The Finnish-Americans' three major publishing centers—Fitchburg, Massachusetts, Superior, Wisconsin, and Calumet, Michigan—published books as well, most of which were socialist. The publishing companies involved were Raivaaja Publishing Company (Fitchburg), Työmis Society (Superior), and Vilho Leikas & Company (Calumet). The last of these published a three-volume translation of Ingersoll's works in 1906. Raivaaja Publishing Company published a series of bound Ingersoll lectures in 1907.

The Swedish-Americans had several socialist societies which were anti-clerical (and especially anti-Lutheran). Their freethought publications were *Forskaren* (Minneapolis, 1893-1924), *Frihetsklocken* (Chicago, 1892-1895), *Rothuggaren* (Litchfield and Grove City, Minnesota, 1880-1886), and *Upplysningens Tidehvarf* (Hutchinson, Glencoe, and Grove City, Minnesota, 1877-1881). Some of the more socialist papers, steeped in anti-clericalism, were *Svenska Socialisten* (Chicago, 1909-1921), *Svenska Arbeitaren* (Chicago, 1882-1884), *Fylgia* (Chicago, 1907-1909), and *Gnistan* (Minneapolis, 1891-1892). There was also an anti-religious anarchist monthly called *Revolt* (Chicago, 1911-1916). Other publications were *Bytingen* (Chicago, circa 1902-1912); *Wak-Upp,* a socialist monthly (Chicago and Evanston, Illinois, 1905-1907); *Glimtar,* an annual (Chicago, 1916 and possibly later); *Svenska Weckobladet,* a weekly (Omaha and Council Bluffs, Iowa, and then in Kansas City, Missouri, and Kansas, 1884-1891; *Facklan* which directly or indirectly superseded *Svenska Weckobladet,* (Kansas City, Missouri, 1891-1892, and Chicago, 1894-1895); and *Ny Tid,* a socialist monthly (Chicago, 1910-1915).

The only Danish-American publication (other than the Norwegian/Danish *Den Nye Tid* mentioned under the Norwegian listings) was *Tilskueren,* which was primarily a socialist monthly newspaper (Chicago, 1878-1882).

Italian-American freethought was closely related to the socialist movement. One of the strongest strains of the Italian-American movement was its pronounced anti-clericalism. Aspects of this anti-clericalism are discussed in the pamphlet by "Agatodemon" called *Dalla Propaganda Anticlericale alla Propaganda Antireligiosa* (Buffalo: Tipgrafia Cooperativa Italiana, 1909).

The Italian-Americans' major socialist/anti-clerical periodicals were the weekly newspapers *La Parola dei Socialiste* (Chicago, 1908-1914, then published under the name of *La Parola Proletaria,* 1914-

1917) and *Il Proletario* (New York, 1899-1946, with a name change to *La Difesa* in 1918 and to *Il Nouvo Proletario* from 1918 to 1920). There was also *La Nouva Luche* (Cleveland, 1899-1910). Around 1908, the movement had a freethought/anti-clerical club in Chicago called the Circulo Giordano Bruno. It published the *Tribuna Italia.*

The Italian-Americans also had a large anarchist movement which was often highly anti-clerical and atheistic. The publications of the anarchist movement are outside the scope of this book, and the number and complexity of their publishing history is so vast, that we will not mention them here. Suffice it to say that there were two anti-religious pamphlets that were widely reprinted (as pamphlets and as magazine and newspaper articles) in the anarchist media, even though they both originated abroad. These were *The God Pest* (or *Pestilence*) by Johann Most (1846-1906) and Sebastian Faure's *Does God Exist?* Versions of these pamphlets were published in America in Italian (as well as in several other languages).

The problem of describing the Yiddish freethought publications in the United States is quite complex. There were a large number of Yiddish language publications in New York, Chicago, and Boston around 1900; many of which were politically radical (i.e., socialist, anarchist, or communist). Publications of this type, especially in Yiddish, tended to be anti-clerical, atheistic, and rationalistic. However, these philosophies were so intertwined that it is impossible to call a publication just "freethought" or just "socialist," for example. Most of these Yiddish publications have not been previously described by anyone as to their *religious* outlook, other than to say that they were anti-religious in general. It can safely be stated that most, if not all, of the politically radical publications were also against the *Jewish* religion. Most took the next logical step and turned against organized religion in general.

Among the publications fitting our criteria were *Arbeiter Zeitung* (New York, 1890-1902), *Freie Arbeiter Stimme* (New York, 1890-1894, and 1899 to the present), *Forward* (New York, 1897 to the present), *Naye Zeit* (New York, 1886), *New Yorker Yiddisher Volkzeitung* (New York, 1886-1889), *Zukunft* (New York, 1892 to the present), *The Morning Freiheit* (New York, 1922 and afterwards), *Warheit* (New York, 1889 onward), *Di Naye Tsayt* (New York, 1886 only), *The Truth* (New York, 1889 only), and *Der Morgenstern* (New York, 1890 only). Those periodicals that are still being published usually modified their anti-religious position after the 1930s.

Additional New York City publications of this type were *Yiddisher Arbeiter* (1931-1932), *Der Union Arbeiter* (1926-1927), *Unser Haver* (1926- ?), *Fortschrift* (1915- ?), *Der Freund* (1910-

1962?), *Der Gerechtigkeit* (1919-1955), *Der Hammer* (1926-1939), *Ikor* (1925), *Jugend* (1926-1927), *Jugandfan* (1926), *Der Pioneer* (1925), *Der Wecker* (1921-1935, 1936 to the present), *Brooklyner Naye Zeitung* (1909), *Yiddisher Socialistische Monatschrift* (1920-1922), and the *Yiddisher Jahrbuch,* an annual, (1914-1918).

Chicago's Yiddish language radical publications were *Die Yiddisher Arbeiter Welt* (1908-1917), which then became called *Die Welt* (1917-1919), and was finally renamed *Forward* (1919 to the present). There were also *Prolitarisrher Gedanke* (1924 onward), *Die Freie Gesellschaft* (1895-1910), *Unser Vort* (1915-1918), *Der Nayer Dor* newspaper: 1905; magazine: 1913-1916), and *Freie Jungnt* (1917).

In the Boston area, there were *Yiddisher Fuhrer* (1923), *Das Naye Vort* (1914), *Der Emes* (1895-1899), and *Jugend Stimme* (1927).

The Ukranians, Hungarians, Spanish, French, Russians, Armenians, blacks, and Irish were also investigated for the existence of free-thought publications in the United States, but we were unable to identify any such publications among them.

APPENDIX II

★ ★ ★ ★ ★ ★ ★ ★ ★ ★

Freethought Collections in U.S. Libraries

This appendix is included because of our own experience in locating copies of particular freethought books and journals. The experience has not been a pleasant one. Very few libraries, even the largest ones, made any effort to acquire freethought books when they were in print, or made any subsequent effort to obtain them as collections, donations, or purchases. There are a few notable exceptions, such as the New York Public Library with its Levy collection and Southern Illinois University with its Ingersoll collection. Of course, the Library of Congress had one advantage over all the other libraries in the United States: it was a copyright depository and thereby obtained two copies of every book copyrighted in the United States. Mostly for this reason, the freethought collection at the Library of Congress (especially of journals) is unsurpassed.

The difficulty in locating copies of a particular book published before 1956 has been greatly lessened by the publication (still not complete) of the *National Union Catalog of Pre-1956 Imprints.* The *National Union Catalog* does not locate collections, however, but only individual titles. It also does not locate papers or manuscripts. There is a *National Union List of Manuscripts,* but it is awkward to use and terribly incomplete.

The information contained in this appendix is the result of a personal investigation of all the institutions listed. Of course, several times as many libraries were checked which did *not* have a significant enough amount of freethought material in their collections to merit a listing at all. Needless to say, it was not possible to visit every library in the United States, and, too, we may have overlooked significant freethought collections. We would be interested in being informed of any such omissions so that we might inspect any other libraries reported to contain good collections.

The description of a given collection as "fine," "good," "fair," and so forth is, of course, a subjective one. Such evaluations were made on the basis of comparative examination of each of the collections listed by one of us (GS), who examined nearly every book the library classified as freethought, via both the card catalog and an actual inspection of the books. Experience with the bibliography of freethought, plus the uniform examination of the collections by the same individual expert, gives us confidence that these evaluations are as fair as possible.

We have encountered a difficult problem in deciding whether to list the names and addresses of individuals who have substantial private freethought collections. This is a matter of some importance as there are several collections in private hands which rival anything in most university libraries. While a number of the individuals involved had no objection to being listed, others did. Therefore, even though these collections contain some unique freethought materials, we have decided not to identify these collectors publicly. However, we will make their identities and addresses available on an individual basis to scholars who have a legitimate research need for these materials. These scholars may obtain this information by writing to Dr. Stein in care of the publisher.

The following list of library freethought collections is arranged geographically, with each of the states listed alphabetically.

California

1. UCLA (Los Angeles): a fair general freethought collection.
2. Huntington Library (San Marino): the papers of British freethinker Richard Carlile.

Connecticut

1. Yale University (New Haven): a good collection on British freethought, with especially good journal coverage; weaker on American freethought.
2. Wesleyan University (Middletown): the Beals collection on British labor history, which contains much freethought material.

District of Columbia

1. Library of Congress: the best freethought periodical holdings in the United States and a fine collection of freethought books, mostly in very good condition; the bulk of Robert G. Ingersoll's papers.
2. Georgetown University: a small collection of Ingersoll papers.

Illinois

1. Illinois State Historical Society (Springfield): a large collection of Robert G. Ingersoll's papers.

2. Northwestern University (Evanston): a fair collection of general freethought materials; the Kaye Deism collection (strong on Deism); the Wright collection on the history of religion/occult/witchcraft.

3. Southern Illinois University (Carbondale): a very large collection of books by and about Robert G. Ingersoll, including some of his papers; the papers and most of the books of Theodore Schroeder; the files of the Open Court Publishing Company.

4. University of Chicago (Chicago): a good general freethought collection, especially strong on George Jacob Holyoake, the British freethinker.

5. University of Illinois (Champaign/Urbana): the Baskette collection on Freedom of Expression, which contains a fair amount of freethought material.

Kansas

1. Kansas State College (Pittsburg): the papers and publications of E. Haldeman-Julius and his Little Blue Book Company.

Maryland

1. University of Maryland (College Park): a fair general freethought collection.

Massachusetts

1. Harvard University (Cambridge): a very good general freethought collection; a fairly good collection of freethought periodicals; the papers of Francis Ellingwood Abbot in the Archives.

2. American Antiquarian Society (Worcester): many early editions of U.S. freethought publications, such as *The Age of Reason;* a complete file of *The Boston Investigator.*

Michigan

1. University of Michigan (Ann Arbor): a good general freethought collection; much freethought material in the Labadie Collection on Social Protest Movements.

Minnesota

1. University of Minnesota (Minneapolis/St. Paul): a good collection of ethnic freethought materials in its Immigration History Research Center.

New Jersey

1. Princeton University (Princeton): a fair general freethought book collection.

2. Rutgers University (New Brunswick): a fair general freethought book collection.

New York

1. Columbia University (New York City): a good general freethought book collection, with many volumes of bound pamphlets.

2. New York Public Library (Reference Division, New York City): the Irving Levy collection, which consists of hundreds of bound volumes of freethought pamphlets—probably the largest such collection in the United States; a good general collection of freethought books and good periodical holdings in freethought.

3. Union Theological Seminary (New York City): the McAlpin collection on British Deism, probably the largest in the United States on this subject; some other freethought material.

North Carolina

1. Duke University (Durham): in its Divinity School library a fair collection of freethought material. (Not actually seen by present compiler.)

Ohio

1. Ohio State University (Columbus): a fair collection of freethought materials.

Pennsylvania

1. American Philosophical Society (Philadelphia): the Gimbel collection on Thomas Paine, probably the best in existence.

2. University of Pennsylvania (Philadelphia): the Lea collection of materials on the Inquisition and on witchcraft.

Texas

1. University of Texas (Austin): a fair general freethought collection. (Not actually seen by present compiler.)

Wisconsin

1. University of Wisconsin (Madison): a good general freethought collection; very strong in British freethought materials, purchased from David Collis.

2. Wisconsin State Historical Society (Madison): many of Theodore Schroeder's books (mostly freethought); much material on the German freethought societies (Freie Gemeinden).

One private collection, the library of the Truth Seeker Company in San Diego, California, is open to the public upon advance application. Application to use the library should be made to Mr. James Hervey Johnson, P.O. Box 2832, San Diego, Calif. 92112. The library contains over 1,000 volumes of books and pamphlets, plus a complete file of *The Truth Seeker* magazine.

APPENDIX III

* * * * * * * * * *

Theses and Dissertations
on Freethought

The following are unpublished dissertations and theses on freethought history or biography. Theses or dissertations subsequently published as books (e.g., Sidney Warren's *American Freethought, 1860-1914*) are not listed here, but rather in the body of this book as one of the references. The entries are alphabetical by author and include only material on freethought in the United States (even though there have been a number of excellent unpublished dissertations on British freethought).

Ahlstrom, Sidney E. "Francis Ellingwood Abbot: His Education and Active Career." Ph.D. Dissertation, Harvard University, 1951.

Brewster, Harold Leland. "An Objective Study of the Oratory of Robert Green Ingersoll." Ph.D. Dissertation, University of Southern California, 1940.

Brudnoy, David. "Liberty's Bugler: The Seven Ages of Theodore Schroeder." Ph.D. Dissertation, Brandeis University, 1971.

Bushman, Charles Henry. "The Ethos of Robert Green Ingersoll." M.A. Thesis, Long Beach State College, 1963.

Callaghan, William J. "Philosophy of Francis E. Abbot." Ph.D. Dissertation, Columbia University, 1958.

Cothran, Andrew. "The Little Blue Book Man and the American Parade: A Biography of Emanuel Haldeman-Julius." Ph.D. Dissertation, University of Maryland, 1966.

De Cordova, June E. "A Study of the Style of Selected Speeches of Robert Green Ingersoll." M.A. Thesis, University of Michigan, 1942.

DeKay, Sam Hoffman. "An American Humanist: The Religious Thought of Francis Ellingwood Abbot." Ph.D. Dissertation, Columbia University, 1977.

Fisher, Raymond Louis. "The Rhetorical Principles of Robert Green Ingersoll." Ph.D. Dissertation, University of Illinois, 1968.

French, Roderick Stuart. "The Trials of Abner Kneeland—A Study in the Rejection of Democratic Secular Humanism." Ph.D. Dissertation, George Washington University, 1971.

Hartnett, James Richard. "The Origin and Growth of the Ethical Culture Movement in the United States." Ph.D. Dissertation, St. Louis University, 1958.

Herder, Dale. "Education for the Masses: The Haldeman-Julius Little Blue Books as Popular Culture During the Nineteen-Twenties." Ph.D. Dissertation, Michigan State University, 1975.

Jensen, J. Vernon. "The Rhetoric of Thomas H. Huxley and Robert G. Ingersoll in Relation to the Conflict Between Science and Religion." Ph.D. Dissertation, University of Minnesota, 1959.

Kincaid, Gerald L. "The 'Lines of Argument' Used by Robert G. Ingersoll in His Lectures on Religion. M.A. Thesis, University of Illinois, 1941.

Kleber, John E. "The Magic of His Power: Robert G. Ingersoll and His Day." Ph.D. Dissertation, University of Kentucky, 1969.

Krumbein, Aaron. "The Social Philosophy of Robert Ingersoll." M.A. Thesis, Columbia University, 1943.

McDowell, Jean Thelma. "Elements of Effective Oratorical Style Found in the Lectures of Robert G. Ingersoll." M.A. Thesis, Northwestern University, 1930.

Prillaman, Lexro Bernard. "Figures of Speech in the Lectures of R. G. Ingersoll." M.A. Thesis, Northwestern University, 1931.

Ranson, Allan O. "The Persuasive Methods of Robert G. Ingersoll." M.A. Thesis, University of Wisconsin, 1935.

Rivers, Fred M. "Francis Ellingwood Abbot: Free Religionist and Cosmic Philosopher." Ph.D. Dissertation, University of Maryland, 1970.

Roberts, Robert Rewalt. "Freethought Movement of Chicago." M.A. Thesis, University of Chicago, 1947.

Seabury, Hugh F. "Typical Deliberative and Demonstrative Speeches of Robert Green Ingersoll: A Comparative Study in Arrangement." M.A. Thesis, University of Iowa, 1933.

Thompson, Donald Claude. "Robert G. Ingersoll and the Freethought Press." M.S. Thesis, University of Wisconsin, 1952.

Tishler, Hace. "Robert Ingersoll." M.A. Thesis, Columbia University, 1959.

Victor, Viggo Florian. "A Study of the Sources and Use of Historical and Literary Materials in the Speeches of Robert Green Ingersoll." M.S. Thesis, Northwestern University, 1934.

Wiltsee, Herbert. "Robert G. Ingersoll, A Study in Religious Liberalism." Ph.D. Dissertation, University of Chicago, 1941.

APPENDIX IV

★ ★ ★ ★ ★ ★ ★ ★ ★

Canadian Freethought

An extraordinarily small amount of freethought activity occurred in Canada—such a small amount in fact that it can be adequately covered in this short appendix.

While visiting Canada in 1882, Charles Watts, a British freethought lecturer and publisher, impressed the members of the Toronto Secular Society, which had been formed in 1873. They invited him to come to Canada, bringing his family, and set up a magazine and be a free-thought lecturer to the Society. Watts agreed and arrived with his family in 1884.

In 1885, he began publishing *Secular Thought* from Toronto. Watts also issued (in many cases, reissued) a number of his own writings, most of which were the texts of his lectures. Some had been published earlier in England. Charles Watts returned to England in 1891, and J. Spencer Ellis carried on publication of *Secular Thought*. The magazine lasted until 1911.

Captain Robert Chamblett Adams was the leader and main force behind the Montreal Pioneer Freethought Club for many years. The Club was founded in 1880 and lasted until about 1903. Adams wrote several books, which were all published in the United States. *Good Without God* (New York: Peter Eckler, [1902]) and his autobiography, *Travels in Faith from Tradition to Reason* (New York: G.P. Putnam's Sons, 1884), are his principal works.

Alan Pringle, a supporter of Robert G. Ingersoll, published several pamphlets, among them *Ingersoll in Canada* (Napanee, Ontario: Standard Book and Job Co., 1880), after the appearance of some newspaper articles criticizing Ingersoll.

Several times during the early 1900s, the Canadian postal authorities prohibited entry of *The Truth Seeker* (343) into Canada. The ban was later lifted without any further legal action being taken against the prohibited issues.

Addendum

A number of books on freethought have been published since the numbering system of this bibliography was completed. In addition, several books have been announced for publication but have not as yet appeared. Finally, we have discovered a few useful works we missed before. This section therefore contains such items.

A1. Angeles, Peter, ed. *Critiques of God.* Buffalo, N.Y.: Prometheus Books, 1977.
A2. Blanshard, Paul, ed. *Classics of Free Thought.* Buffalo, N.Y.: Prometheus Books, 1977.
A3. Carter, Lee. *Lucifer's Handbook—A Simplified Critique of Popular Religion.* (Los Angeles): Academic Associates, 1977. A compendium of the arguments for and against the existence of God.
A4. Eddy, Richard. *Universalism in America.* Boston: Universalist Publishing House, 1886, 2 vols. Remarkable for its 116 page, 2200+ item bibliography on Universalism.
A5. Greeley, Roger E., ed. *Ingersoll: Immortal Infidel.* Buffalo, N.Y.: Prometheus Books, 1978.
A6. Menendez, Albert J. *Church-State Relations: An Annotated Bibliography.* New York: Garland Publishing, 1976.
A7. Ryan, William F. *Haldeman-Julius and the Blue Academy.* Buffalo, N.Y.: Prometheus Books, announced as "forthcoming" in 1978.
A8. Sears, Hal D. *The Sex Radicals: Free Love in High Victorian America.* Lawrence, Kans.: Regents Press of Kansas, 1977. Contains much information on D. M. Bennett, Elmina Slenker, R. G. Ingersoll, and other freethinkers.
A9. Wilbur, Earl Morse. *A History of Unitarianism in Transylvania, England and America.* Cambridge, Mass.: Harvard University Press, 1952. Perhaps the best study of early Unitarianism in the United States.

Glossary of Terms

Agnosticism   The belief which holds that the ultimate cause (God) and the essential nature of things are, by their very nature, unknown and unknowable. The agnostic would say that such knowledge is impossible for mankind to ever obtain.

Atheism   The lack of belief in, or disbelief in, the existence of God. The denial of God's existence, while a form of atheism, is not necessary for an atheistic outlook. Atheism is really just a state of being without theism.

Deism   The belief (based solely upon reason) that God was the creator of the universe, but that He abandoned it and assumed no control over it after setting it in motion. The Deist would say that God now has no control over life, no influence over natural phenomena, and that he gave men no supernatural revelation. A Deist, therefore, would believe in God's existence, but would not believe in prayer, the Bible, Jesus as Messiah, or the truth of any organized religion.

Freethinker   One who has rejected authority and dogma, especially in his religious thinking, in favor of rational inquiry.

Freethought   (sometimes written "free thought")   Thought which is free of dogmatic assumptions (usually religious dogmas), and which seeks the answers to all questions through rational inquiry.

Humanism   The viewpoint that men have but one life to lead, and that they should make the most of it in tems of creative work and happiness. The idea that human happiness is its own justification and requires no sanction or support from supernatural sources. The idea that, in any case, the supernatural does not exist, and that human beings, using their own intelligence and cooperating liberally with one another, can build an enduring citadel of peace and beauty upon this earth. (Corliss Lamont)

Iconoclast   One who attacks and seeks to overthrow traditional or popular ideas or institutions. Literally, an "idol smasher."

Infidel   One who has no belief in organized religion. Sometimes applied to those who do not believe in a *particular* religion, such as Christianity.

Liberalism   A movement in modern Protestantism which emphasizes freedom from tradition and authority and the adjustent of religious beliefs to scientific conceptions.

Rationalism (as applied to religious controversy)   The doctrine that human reason, unaided by divine revelation, is an adequate guide, or the sole guide, to all attainable religious truth.

Secularist   One who believes that public education and other matters of civil policy and government should be conducted without the introduction of a religious element.

Transcendentalism   The belief that knowledge of reality is derived from intuitive sources rather than from objective experience.

Unitarianism   A Christian denomination which, in general, affirms the principles of individual freedom of belief, the free use of reason in religion, commitment to advancing truth, religious tolerance, universal brotherhood of man, a creedless church, a united world community, and support of a vigorous program of liberal social action.

Universalism   A Christian denomination which believes that all men will finally be saved. Since God is love, Universalists reasoned that God would not be satisfied with either everlasting punishment or partial salvation. In the twentieth century, the beliefs of Universalism became very similar to those of Unitarianism (no exact creed required). The two churches merged in 1961.

Author and Person Index

This index contains the names of all the persons mentioned in this book, whether as an author or in any other context.

Title Index

Names of magazines and newspapers are italicized. Titles of books are in roman. Titles of magazine articles, titles of lectures, titles of a chapter in a book or part of a book, and titles of dissertations are in quotation marks.

Subject Index

ABOUT THE AUTHORS

Marshall G. Brown, a former secondary school principal and super-
visor of adult education, has studied the history of freethought for
more than forty years. He is the author of *Genealogy of the Harvey
Family of Garrett County, Maryland* and has prepared a bibliographic
series for the *American Rationalist*.

Gordon Stein is a physiologist and editor. His interest in freethought
extends over ten years, and has resulted in what is one of the largest
collections of freethought books in private hands. His publications include *Robert G. Ingersoll: A Checklist* and numerous articles for scholarly journals. He is at work on a history of blasphemy prosecutions.